3 Second Rule:

How to Trust Your Instinct

ISBN: 1508964246
ISBN 13: 9781508964247

Dedication

To everyone who sees the value in growing more confident in their decisions, actions, and outcomes.

Table of Contents

Other Books by Douglas Shawn Blakeny II

The Investment (fiction)
Shock-Up (fiction, to be released)

3 Second Rule:

How to Trust Your Instinct

by Douglas Shawn Blakeny II

Introduction

We all experience conflict when our logical left brains clash with our spontaneous, heartfelt right brains. The way we resolve this conflict is fundamental to how our brains process decisions. *Everything* is impacted by it.

Far too many of us are disconnected from our instincts, despite their necessity in our lives. Instincts are especially important if we desire to live optimally — to our greatest potential. Instincts are linked to our subconscious, and are our greatest source of judgment. Furthermore, they quickly assist us in making a decision. *In fact, we can make one within three seconds.* The caveat: They only work for us if we allow them to.

Why follow your instincts? The answer is clear. They do not involve the following:

- ✓ Intensive Evaluation
- ✓ Overanalysis
- ✓ Hesitation

Perhaps your instinct tells you that evaluation is wise. If so, consider this explanation:

Instincts can compel action and inspire us. Will we make mistakes? Of course. We are human beings, designed imperfectly and created to grow and evolve as our lives unfold. But the process of developing the "right instincts" is timeless. It's a part of who we are; a way to move forward in life with confidence and grace.

Instincts are important to me. I have devoted considerable time and attention to honing my own instincts, and other people can do the same. It's not as hard as you think: You only need to bring out what already exists in your right brain, instead of creating something new for your left brain to overanalyze (which it loves to do so much). I know that accurate instincts can be achieved — if you have a commitment to success.

Who Is This Book For?

The simple answer to the question is *everyone*. This book is for everyone. The younger we can begin using our instincts and the longer we maintain them, the better off we are. We will be better able to take corrective action, and everything will get easier, both on a personal and professional level.

Let's consider why this book is essential for everyone.

If you possess any of these negative thought patterns, you are currently not in a position for intuitive thinking to work for your greater good:

- ✓ You tend to excessively evaluate everything before you take action.
- ✓ You constantly fear that you're going to make the wrong decision.
- ✓ You believe you will be better off if you follow a detailed, thoughtfully laid-out process about how to make every important move in your life.
- ✓ You hypothesize that if an opportunity passes you by, it wasn't meant to be.
- ✓ You feel your life is stagnant, while everyone else's life is moving forward and upward.
- ✓ You feel ill-equipped to take control of your life, and you can't make the simplest decisions.
- ✓ You find yourself thinking that you're not effective at making good decisions for your own life and wellbeing.

These thoughts can stop today. This book is going to help you take corrective action, so you can go from overanalysis to the liberation of intuitively based decisions.

An Overview of the 3 Second Rule

When we transition away from intensive, ego-driven decision-making and revert to our instincts, we begin living according to the 3 Second Rule. With this rule, we gain the confidence to make stronger, better decisions. The more we rely on our instincts, the more confident we'll become at handing them back over to our subconscious.

We fire our ego! And it is liberating!

Once the 3 Second Rule becomes our primary mode of decision-making, we are able to devote more time and attention to what's around us. It's a profound, transformational change that will help improve the outcomes of our entire lives.

What Is This Book Designed to Do for You?

Imagine the power of making a sound decision in 3 seconds or less. It's an exhilarating feeling, I assure you!

Each chapter in this book is a building block that will help you improve your strategies for navigating your life. You'll learn a better way, which will allow you to use positive energy and the power of thought to create a more fulfilling life. This new life will help you accomplish your dreams and exude your potential *with* your right instincts intact.

You will go through a series of steps, which will help you home in on specific areas of your life. Then you can acknowledge, strengthen, and envision a more powerful way of living.

Here are the building blocks:

✓ **Establish your starting point.**
   Through a thoughtful, honest evaluation of your current approach to decisions and actions in your life, you can better understand who you are as a

person. Knowledge and self-awareness are essential for beginning the process of building the right instincts.

✓ **Take the bold step of acknowledgment.**
With a truthful evaluation of what you say, what you do, and what you feel, you can begin to acknowledge the patterns of how you think and respond.

✓ **Understand how you choose to take action.**
We all take action (or inaction, which is also a choice) in different ways. Are you active, passive, or fearful? You may be active in one area, but fearful in another. So we'll also evaluate the *context* of your actions. (We'll cover the difference between passivity and fear in Chapter 3.)

✓ **Be comfortable with being self-aware.**
Many people are not comfortable in their own skin, and that has to change. It's very liberating to understand who we are and admit it to ourselves. But it takes confidence, awareness of ourselves and our surroundings, and the conscious act of establishing goals that are geared toward overcoming our weaknesses — whether real or perceived. This process will help our brains transition into a better way of processing information.

✓ **Capitalize on your desires.**
When we desire something, we naturally gain a sense of excitement, energy, and ambition. We want it to come true. So learning how to use desire to fuel our motivations and drives is a very beneficial life step.

✓ **<u>Build up your drive.</u>**

We need a way to drive our spiritual, emotional, and physical machines. Without this drive, we will be thrown off by the first thing that goes wrong. When we encounter obstacles in our lives, we need something to keep us resilient, motivated, and on course. Often, when we encounter obstacles, our ego manifests as hesitation, inaction, or self-doubt.

✓ **<u>Examine your principles and values.</u>**

In order to have authentic, positively directed discipline, we must take into account what our principles and values truly are. You can transition into something you are currently not, but you must be invested in the change. Don't think you can simply force the change on your psyche.

✓ **<u>Embrace self-evaluation.</u>**

It is hard to give ourselves an honest evaluation. It is not easy to admit where we may have fallen short of our expectations. To make the most out of self-evaluation, you need to develop practical and applicable thought processes that lead to doable actions.

✓ **<u>Find fulfillment.</u>**

When we experience fulfillment, we come to recognize the value of rewards, visions, and internal peace. You may not understand exactly what fulfillment is at the current moment, and that's okay. If you'd like to understand it a bit more, think of someone you know that always seems to have a sense of harmony and ease about them — someone who remains unruffled by distractions, and is tried and true. This person uses the 3 Second Rule in some capacity.

When we go through the above experiences in an aware manner, we begin to learn what we seek. Each chapter of this book is going to assist in that search, and will include techniques and concepts that will help you create intuitive habits. They will serve your interests well, while transforming you into an individual who lives a 3 Second Rule way of life. Each chapter will have additional stories and scenarios that help with a particular building block. These stories will illustrate how the chapter will assist the transformation you seek. They paint vivid pictures that bring things to life, because they're real people's experiences.

Transitioning to the 3 Second Rule

The first question most people have after taking the time to work on the building blocks that bridge the gap between them and their intuition is this: How will I know that I've grown, and that my intuition is working for me?

You'll notice three attributes in your internal dialogue, as well as in your external actions:

✓ **Trust:** Both in yourself and your decisions.

✓ **Effortlessness:** Both stressful evaluation and self-doubt lessen, and an innate knowledge grows that you can make correct decisions.

✓ **Acceptance:** Embrace the fact that your intuition is just as qualified to guide you as your conscious, ego-driven willpower. Your intuition intimately and profoundly taps into who you are.

At that point, you will have come full-circle and begun living a life that once seemed like a utopian fantasy.

To help ensure that this life happens, this book has a plan of action to work with you and help you grow into an active, practicing participant of the 3 Second Rule. Why should you believe in this book's promise? Because you will experience how it works firsthand. You are the next story of success!

At the end of this book, there is a section to help you master the different stages: **3 steps** for **3 months** that lead to **3 Second Rule** results. Admittedly, some people will be more invested in the process and get more out of the experience than others. However, these lessons and concepts are good for anyone in any situation, and are all designed to enhance the outcome of your life's decisions.

By thinking outside the box, you can find approaches to betterment that offer the wonderful potential to tap into the answers that exist within you. You've been ignoring your instincts all these years. Make it up to them by acknowledging their existence, and finally listening to their guidance! Listening to your instincts is a game-changer, and that's what excites me most about sharing this book with you.

CHAPTER ONE

Your Starting Point

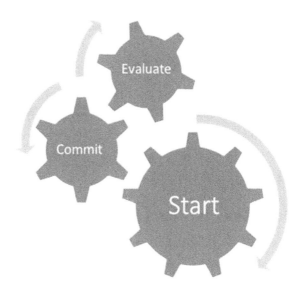

If we just make an effort to determine where we truly are in this life — at this exact moment — we can start turning our mental cogs. If we commit to this process in a thoughtful manner, the internal machine that controls our instincts will get fired up and start helping us recognize the problems in our lives. Once we do that, we can begin to address problems, and maybe even solve them.

Ask yourself the following questions: What do you do that continuously stops you in your tracks? How do your decisions turn out? Why do you make the choices you make? By asking yourself these questions, you can start making a thoughtful evaluation of your life. And that is the beginning of change. It truly does not matter where you are starting from. Starting is enough.

The 3 Second Rule Quiz

Before you move on to the remaining chapters, I recommend taking the following quiz. By thoughtfully evaluating your life, you can become more aware. In turn, this process will help you create a better dialogue for taking on the building blocks in the following chapters.

Directions for the Quiz

If you have the book in print, feel free to write in it directly, as it will likely become a valuable companion, and guide you to make the changes you want. Just knowing that you made this exciting, transformational purchase shows your commitment to wanting something more — something better — for your life.

Here are some suggestions to help make the process of taking the quiz more enjoyable:

✓   Be relaxed when you do it.

- ✓ Don't do it in a rush.
- ✓ Drop everything else to give yourself the time to focus on you.
- ✓ Be honest, because you can't build authentic adjustments to your intuition without being honest.
- ✓ Allow yourself to experience enthusiasm.
- ✓ Grant yourself forgiveness whenever you find it necessary.

There are no right or wrong answers to any of these questions. They also aren't "gotcha" questions. Their sole purpose is to help guide you in what you currently do, and assist you with recognizing how it has worked out for you. You'll have strengths and weaknesses, as we all do. SWOT is an acronym in the business world. It's a process for evaluating the following:

- ✓ **S**trengths: What assets do you have to work with?

- ✓ **W**eaknesses: How could you use improvements?

- ✓ **O**pportunities: What can you leverage?

- ✓ **T**hreats: What things hold you back?

That's what this book will allow you to do, because there's no business as wonderful as the "You Business."

Enjoy!

The Quiz

1. Do you believe that your life can be easy, and that you can still do everything you want?
   a. Yes
   b. No

2. How aware are you of what you're genuinely feeling at any moment?
   a. I know, but if I don't want to deal with it, I avoid it.
   b. I just go with the flow, not really paying attention to much more than that.
   c. I am the most confused person I know.
   d. Honestly, I have no idea. I don't really focus on that type of thing very often.

3. When you think about the current level of trust you have in your decision-making abilities, which of these choices seems most accurate?
   a. I always run into trouble by making the wrong choice.
   b. My ability to make a sound choice is pretty decent.
   c. More often than not, I talk myself into trusting the choices I make.
   d. I just do what I want, and don't put much thought into it.

How do you feel about your answer? Do you like or dislike it? Why?

_____

_____

4. Something <u>urgent</u> needs to be done. What are you most likely to do?
    a. Take care of it immediately. After all, it needs your attention.
    b. Put it on your priority list in the proper place, according to the order in which you want to deal with it.
    c. Procrastinate, for whatever reason.
    d. Dwell and contemplate, but don't act for a long time. If it's urgent, you want to take your time.

5. Something that's <u>not urgent</u> needs to be done. What are you most likely to do?
    a. Put it off as long as you can.
    b. Do it right away, because it's not challenging.
    c. Keep forgetting about it. There are too many other fires to put out.
    d. Put it in the proper spot on your priority list.

How do you feel about the differences between urgent and non-urgent actions?

_____

_____

6. You're faced with a task, and there are two ways to do it. Choice One is the easy way: You're cutting a few

corners, but saving a ton of time. Choice Two is to do it the right way, so you don't ever have to go back and do it again. What will you choose to do most often?

a. Choice One: Get it done. And if it comes back to bite you, you'll deal with it then.

b. Choice Two: Do it right the first time, and move on to the next thing.

If you selected Choice One, what outcome usually happens? And how do you feel about it?

_____

_____

7. Something new comes up in your life. You have to decide if you're going to pursue it, or take a pass. How do you feel about your ability to evaluate your decision-making process?

a. Pretty great. I analyze it, do research, sleep on it, and do a second run-through. Then I'm set for action.

b. If I have any hesitation, it's an automatic no.

c. If it sounds interesting, I'm all in.

d. I say yes right away. Then I dive into the details later, especially if it involves a financial gain of some sort.

8. When I want something really badly and can't stop thinking about it, I:

a. Create a plan to obtain it, then obtain it.

b. Create a plan to obtain it, but usually lose interest along the way.

c. Dwell on it and daydream about it, but don't ever really "go for it."

d. Think it's such a long shot that it's not worth my time. Case closed.

When was the last time you got something that you really desired, either big or small? How did that feel for you?

_____

_____

9. How far are you willing to go in life to get what you want?

a. The distance.

b. Not too far.

c. Far enough to see if it's worth it.

d. I'm too busy to even consider pursuing most things.

10. Having discipline isn't easy at times, and it can present a challenge, even to the most successful individual. What about you? What do you do?

a. Feel that it's okay to take some time off and recharge.

b. Make sure I work toward what I want every day, regardless of what else occurs.

c. Find it easy to be disciplined when I'm busy, but not as easy when I don't have a full schedule.

Evaluate your disciplinary behaviors. Regarding discipline, what are your strengths, and where could you use some improvement?

_____

_____

11. When you think about yourself, what do you do?
    a. Focus on failures first, then successes.
    b. Focus on successes, then the lessons learned from failures.
    c. Only think about the failures.
    d. Only think about the successes.

12. If you were giving advice to a friend who had identical mannerisms to you, what would you do?
    a. Be very kind to them, even if it wasn't the best advice.
    b. Be direct and gentle, and really try to be helpful, even if it's tough.
    c. Just listen and let them talk it out themselves.
    d. Tell them what you think they should do, directly and without exception.

In your own experience, how do you feel about offering advice? And how about receiving it, both solicited and unsolicited?

_____

_____

13. Regardless of how busy you are, do you feel that what you do leads to a more fulfilling life?
    a. All the time. I love the life I've chosen, bumps and joys alike.
    b. Most of the time. But there are times when I have to wonder: *What was I thinking?*
    c. Never. I've gotten it wrong so many times that I'm not even sure what being right feels like anymore.
    d. Thinking about it is too irritating, so I choose not to.

14. What would you do if everything started going your way — to the point where you couldn't ignore that things were "clicking"?
    a. Wonder when it's going to end.
    b. Seize the day.
    c. Hide out, for fear the sky is falling.
    d. Think it's a cruel joke.

That wasn't so bad, was it? Now it's time to find out *exactly* where you are at this moment in time. Keep in mind that the smallest strides toward building the bridge to your intuition can significantly change your life. Just as the ripples from tossing a pebble into the water grow bigger, so does the smallest change that takes you one step closer to your intuition.

Your Intuitive Starting Point

By determining where you're starting from, you've already taken a significant step toward your power source: your intuition. Don't worry about where you fall on the rating scale at this point, because everyone has room for improvement. Also, while you may have been as honest as you could be, self-evaluation is inherently difficult at the beginning.

These pages contain a path that will help you succeed. When you add up your score, don't count the write-in questions. They're simply meant to establish your starting point for building intuition.

First, add up your score, based on the following values for each question:

1. a-2; b-1
2. a-4; b-3; c-2; d-1
3. a-1; b-3; c-2; d-4
4. a-3; b-4; c-2; d-1
5. a-1; b-4; c-2; d-3
6. a-2; b-1
7. a-3; b-4; c-1; d-2
8. a-4; b-1; c-3; d-2
9. a-3; b-2; c-4; d-1
10. a-1; b-3; c-2
11. a-3; b-4; c-2; d-1
12. a-1; b-4; c-3; d-2
13. a-3; b-4; c-1; d-2
14. a-3; b-4; c-1; d-2

The maximum number of points that you can get for this quiz is 51. Now I'll explain what your score says about how you currently apply the 3 Second Rule to your life. You may be surprised.

48 and Above: My Bridge is Half-Built
Congratulations, not bad! You have some sound, intuitive building blocks in place. If you get tripped up, it most likely comes from a lack of confidence and a sense of perfectionism.

40 through 47: Riding the Fence
You're onto something, but not quite there. You run about 50/50, in terms of allowing your instincts to work for you. The largest challenge you may face is having a strong self-will, as well as a splash of too much ego.

30 through 39: Belly Flop
You try to get ahead, but more often than not, you accidentally topple over and fall flat on your face. But to your credit, you are someone who will get back up again and maintain hope. You just have to focus on learning from your mistakes and creating an evaluation process.

29 and Below: Build the Ladder Before the Bridge
First, inhale deeply and acknowledge that you have amazing potential for gaining the right instincts. Here is what's lacking: An acceptance of that part of you underneath the surface. It's there; it truly is! As you go through each chapter, take the time to soak in the book's meaning. It's not about rushing to intuition. Instead,

think of it as a meaningful journey that starts the process to bridge that gap and jump-start your life. Exciting stuff!

When my friends have taken this quiz, their reactions and responses have been funny. Some thought they were masterful and intuitive operators in life, but learned that wasn't necessarily the case. They learned they had room to grow. The moral of the story: You just never know, and it can be even worse to just assume.

It's time to dive in and begin building that bridge, but please remember that this journey is self-paced. It's your time, and no one else's. Use it wisely.

CHAPTER TWO

The Art of Acknowledgment

Acknowledgment of your own actions is not always easy. At times, it can be emotionally painful, even embarrassing. The greatest angst comes from times like these: We thought we were making the best choices and giving our best efforts, but we still fell short.

One of the marks of great human beings is the ability to acknowledge what does and doesn't work in our lives. It's a sign of self-awareness, and it's rooted in the understanding that the choices and actions we make toward betterment are never ones that lessen others or hinder their chances. Through selflessness, we can use self-acknowledgment to learn and grow in our lives.

Here's a really touching story I heard, which cements this point:

Veronica was a smart and successful attorney. By most people's standards, she was doing very well, but she was struggling internally. But no one knew about her struggles, and she wasn't willing to admit them.

You see, Veronica was under so much stress that the only time she could relax was late at night, when she got home. Her body would be exhausted, but her mind would be wide awake — thinking about what she had to do the next day, or dwelling on what she hadn't finished before leaving the office. The only way she could relax was by enjoying a glass of wine. I believe we can all agree there's nothing wrong with that. But for Veronica, it grew into a more significant problem. A single glass suddenly turned into two, and then two into three. She'd fall asleep, but wake up exhausted and groggy, muddled from the side effects of the alcohol. That meant she wasn't as productive in the mornings, so she spent even more hours at work.

It was a vicious cycle for Veronica, and it looked like there was no end in sight. But, finally, she was forced to admit that something had to change. She made a significant error on a case, and when people looked to her for answers, she was horrified — really tough on herself. When a senior partner in the firm called her out on it and started asking tough questions, she was fearful. She thought that if she was unable to manage her stress, it might also mean she wasn't fit for her job. But she loved being an attorney, and didn't want to do anything else.

Then the senior partner replied, "Veronica, you do a good job. We see the hours you put in, but something's wrong. What is it?" Of course, these questions have to be asked carefully. Most people don't want to answer them, particularly people in Veronica's situation. However, she was at a turning point. She replied, "I've been working hard. I guess I was just a bit too worn out, and honestly, I made a mistake."

He shook his head. "What do you do to recharge?" Her expression was blank, which revealed quite a bit; she had no idea what to do. That's when he shared some valuable wisdom with Veronica: Everyone needs time to rest their brain and recharge. Longer hours don't necessarily mean better results. He challenged her to take care of herself, to get the escape she needed, and to not think that longer hours at the office always meant better results.

When Veronica left that meeting, she had a lot on her mind. She'd begun to wonder if she had a drinking problem, which was tough to think about. In her eyes, a drinking problem was a weakness.

Veronica was still taking actions to appease others with little regard for herself, but she began going to a kickboxing class at a health club. Three days a week, she gave herself a deadline for leaving the office: 7 PM. It was a start.

The first week was hard, and she missed class twice. The second week, she missed once. And by the third week, she was going all three times, while still completing more work than she had when she'd been staying at the office until 10 PM. Now she had to do what she'd been so resistant to do before: Acknowledge that the best results don't come from forcing yourself to do the most for other people. The best results come from being your best for you!

Today, Veronica is a junior partner, has a healthy and active lifestyle, has created many connections, and has won many cases — all while working an average of ten hours per week less than others in her position. And that glass of wine at the end of the night is the treat she has to celebrate a great day. When her head hits the pillow at night, she knows that she's done well, and that there isn't any urgent matter that she's left unattended at work. And when she wakes up in the morning, she knows that she's got it covered for that day.

This example illustrates the power of acknowledging who we are and where we are operating from.

How about you? Do you see any similarities to your own life in Veronica's story?

When we begin tapping into the art of acknowledgment, there are three central building blocks to consider: What you say, what you do, and what you feel. These building blocks are at the base of everything we acknowledge in life. They show us how we view ourselves through our thoughts, actions, and words.

What Veronica said, what she did, and how she felt offered pivotal bits of information. They helped give her great chances for a better, more balanced life.

As you become more alert in this self-knowledge, things will gradually become more exciting. Imagine that you're trudging through a field, and carrying two large buckets of water that are dangling from a heavy wooden bar across your back. It aches, but you keep going - if you stop, it may be too hard to get going again. So you keep going and going until... you can't anymore. You just don't have it in you.

In the back of your mind, you know that if you'd just admitted it before — acknowledged what your body, mind, and soul were telling you — you could have figured something else out. Or you could at least have taken a needed break on your own accord, rather than it being forced on you.

What Do I Say?

Some people say we are what we eat, but we're also what we say we are. By inwardly or outwardly talking about our shortcomings and faults (or treating ourselves with less dignity than we deserve), we start buying into our own rhetoric, which is dangerous territory.[1]

Furthermore, our negative self-talk provides a buffet of intense, highly unsatisfying emotions, including:

- ✓ Bad feelings about ourselves and/or our lives
- ✓ Simmering feelings of hurt, anger, and frustration
- ✓ Depression and anxiety, or a sense of forlornness

These are horrible emotions — ones that we inherently understand are intensely debilitating. To make matters worse, we start feeling that we are already defeated, and that there is no point in trying. But there is every reason to try!

---

[1] *Taking Charge! A Guide for Teenagers: Practical Ways to Overcome Stress, Hassles and Upsetting Emotions* by Dr. Sarah Edelman and Louise Rémond (2005).

Here are some examples of what negative self-talk sounds like. You may be participating in more of it than you ever imagined:

- ✓ "This is such a long shot. Why waste my time?"
- ✓ "Why bother?"
- ✓ "I'm gonna be stuck here forever."
- ✓ "I probably won't get that raise."
- ✓ "He'll probably take credit for it anyway."
- ✓ "She'll say no, so I'm not going to even try."

When you use negative self-talk, there is no joy, and no ability to lift yourself up. You need to find ways to shift your internal and external dialogue from negative to positive.

Positive self-talk can always trump negative self-talk.

While negative self-talk can weaken you, positive self-talk lifts you up and strengthens you. Simply put, it makes you feel better about yourself and your situation. Then you'll see the light at the end of the tunnel.

The most powerful influences in our lives beckon the confidence we need to trust our intuition. They usually start with the words "I am..."

Negative self-talk often grows at a rapid pace. It's like a weed in a garden. It grows four times quicker than the beautiful things you've planted, eventually strangling them and stomping them out. Positive self-talk is like the sunshine and water that nourishes your emotional garden, and it helps you view things more favorably and act more positively. Here are some examples of positive self-talk:

- ✓ I am capable.
- ✓ I am going to give this a try.
- ✓ I am excited about new opportunities.
- ✓ I am present.
- ✓ I am successful.
- ✓ I trust my intuition, because it looks out for me and my best interests.

You may be thinking, "Well, that's great, D, but how does it relate to the 3 Second Rule?" It relates because building up your intuition has to come from a place of self-love. But your subconscious mind will shy away from self-love if your conscious mind is filled with negative self-talk. If nothing else, please keep in mind how harmful negative self-talk is, and commit to no longer accepting it in your life.

What Do I Do?

We may often feel like no one is paying attention to us, or that what we do does not matter. This feeling is inaccurate. Our actions matter a great deal, and the perceptions we relay through those actions matter a great deal as well. For instance, consider these examples:

- ✓ Our abilities to exert ourselves in a confident, assured manner can lead to professional opportunities.

- ✓ When our self-esteem is favorable, we are more likely to create and cultivate fulfilling personal relationships.
- ✓ People look to others whose actions are favorable as role models and leaders.
- ✓ Our actions impact how we feel about ourselves. As such, negative actions lead to negative feelings, while positive actions lead to increased levels of self-worth.
- ✓ When our actions are positive, we are more closely aligned with our intuitive processes.

<u>Case Study</u>

Tom was a hard worker: Quiet and committed. No one was better than him at taking others' ideas and implementing them in the best possible ways. Also, he didn't complain, which is always appreciated. But he didn't offer any insights either. While some may appreciate that characteristic, it made his coworkers think that Tom didn't have anything to offer that would improve his work environment.

One day after work, Tom went out with a few colleagues for a drink, and they all got to talking. As usual, everyone else talked about their projects, and he just listened, not offering much. But then one woman said something about an idea she had for developing a system to help streamline a process. It sounded familiar, and Tom suggested that she talk to another colleague who'd implemented a similar system. That was the spark that made people wonder a bit more about what Tom knew, and they began asking him question after question. He was full of knowledge, and everyone was eager to learn from him.

As it turned out, Tom had an incredible understanding of all areas of the company (which employed more than 200 people). He knew more about the functions of each department than the president, the owners, or the board. And no one had a clue.

After getting some encouragement from his friends, Tom began to open up more. Once he showed his value, he quickly earned a promotion and became the regional manager. Prior to that, he'd been in the same role for ten years. Had Tom learned anything new? No. He already had the knowledge and skills he needed. The difference was in his actions: He contributed and participated, and the result was favorable — not only to him, but also to the entire organization. (See Chapter 3 for information about obtaining more skills.)

Our actions are what move us forward and help us gain confidence. When we gain confidence, decision-making processes become significantly easier and less time-consuming.

What Do I Feel?

Most of us don't realize exactly how important our emotions are to our perceptions. For instance, there is an internal function called *embodied cognition*, which causes our bodies to respond to our emotions. According to research, love is sweet.[2] Quite literally! When we are in love, food and drink (even distilled water) taste sweeter. Furthermore, researchers believe that this emotional association starts when we're children, particularly for babies who associate breastfeeding and bottles with love.

To me, that information is incredible, and it's something that can profoundly impact our lives. If we didn't feel loved during our childhoods, we can find ways to bridge that gap in our adult lives. We can become more emotionally aware and loving of our wellbeing, which is significant during the pursuit of developing the right type of intuition.

The following emotions and outcomes are linked together:

✓ The desire to feel important is a heavy emotion. Studies show that when someone picks something up, they will estimate how much it weighs by how important it is said to be. Something "insignificant" is considered lighter than something that is deemed "very important."[3] Fascinating! It should be noted that a feeling of powerlessness also makes things seem heavier.

---

[2] Love Really is Sweet, Science Reveals. Pappas, Stephanie. January 21, 2014. http://www.livescience.com/42730-love-really-is-sweet.html.

[3] Just a Touch Can Influence Thoughts and Decisions. Hsu, Jeremy. June 24, 2010. http://www.livescience.com/8360-touch-influence-thoughts-decisions.html.

✓ Loneliness is cold. We feel physically colder, and we feel more emotionally disconnected. This impact leads to significant emotional challenges, which can hinder our inner connections to the things that are best for us.

✓ Being judgmental is tied to the colors black and white. When we are surrounded by these colors, we are more likely to see something as either "is" or "is not." On the other hand, colors tend to promote both sides of the story. This difference is particularly interesting in the context of intuition, because it is much more aligned with black and white. These natural decisions and thought processes are based on instinct, instead of conscious dialogue that's based on the pros and cons of a situation or opportunity.

✓ The perceived temperature of a room is connected with inclusion. People associate inclusion with warmth, whereas they link exclusion with coldness. People associate inclusion with warmth, whereas they link exclusion and cold with each other.

Through the simple act of becoming more aware of how our emotions impact us, we can take great strides toward a better quality of life, which is often a direct result of having a strong amount of intuition. Our physical and emotional beings are intricately linked.

Activating Your Acknowledgment

What do I say? What do I do? What do I feel? By consistently answering these three questions, you will create the first building block in the bridge between your life and your intuition.

In this section, there are areas of focus and activities to help you acknowledge who you are (as you are) at this moment. They will help you envision what you'd like to change, so you can make your life better. These exercises are powerful. They will have a profound impact on your self-perceptions, if you allow them to begin working within you — and for you.

What Do I Say?
Here are a few questions that you should answer about how you speak to others, or even to yourself:

✓ Do you have faith in your ability to solve problems?

_____

✓ In conversation, do you laugh and walk away, feeling good? Or are your conversations dedicated to complaining and thinking about what you don't have?

_____
_____

✓ Are others more responsible for your problems, or are you responsible for them? How do you know the difference?

_____

_____

✓ Think about your last three conversations. How many of them involved negative talk, either about yourself or someone else?

_____

✓ In your conversations with others or in your thoughts about your life, do you focus on adding value?

_____

✓ What part of your life do you find yourself focusing on most: The past, present, or future?

_____

While talking with others, what are your thoughts about the environments you're in?

_____

_____

_____

How do you feel about the messaging of your internal dialogue?

_____

_____

_____

What are three ways you would like to improve your verbal communication?

1. _____
2. _____
3. _____

You know the best ways to get you to commit to change! What are three things that you can do to make your verbal communication more positive?

1. _____
2. _____
3. _____

Now it's time to offer you a few suggestions for positive reinforcement. These items should be definitively positive and helpful. (NOTE: Appendix A has some great information about incorporating affirmations into your daily routine.) As you've already been learning, we often become what we think. So let's accentuate the positive!

Affirmations are precise and to the point. They're only filled with positive and uplifting language, and they're easy to remember. Many people put them all around their environment, or go through a routine that involves repeating them several times a day. It's particularly effective to repeat this process in the mornings. If you're not a morning person, they'll give you an easy pick-me-up, so you can get up and get things done. Here's a few for you to choose from:

- ✓ I've got this.
- ✓ This change is wonderful.
- ✓ I create my own positive world.
- ✓ My destiny is in my hands.
- ✓ Accentuate the positive.

Keep these things in mind, and begin practicing them today. If you're serious about becoming reconnected with your intuition, this practice will be a joy, not just another item on your to-do list. Really, it's a must-do!

<u>What Do I Do?</u>
At the heart of acknowledgment is admitting and accepting what it is that we do or don't do. Our actions tell us so much. Here are some of the things our actions tell us:

- ✓ What we pretend is important to us
- ✓ What we say is important to us
- ✓ What is actually important to us

For example, if someone were to say, "My wish is that no child in my community ever goes hungry," it would be very easy for everyone to agree. However, the real test is in the follow-up. Have you acted on your wish? Or have you just talked the talk? Action has value. Talking only has value if you're trying to inform people, and get them to act with you.

Think about what's of value to you — something you feel passionate about and would love to change. Write it down.

_____

_____

Confession time. List everything that you have actively done to facilitate the change. (Hopefully, you'll need more space than what's offered here!)

_____

_____

Have you done enough to create the change you want?
1. Yes
2. No

Why or why not?

_____

_____

What could you do to start taking action today?

_____

_____

Look at your answer. Did you think about it for a long time, or did you just know? If you just knew, congratulations! Your instincts are working for you on some level. As your instincts activate and launch, you will begin an exciting journey!

<u>What Do I Feel?</u>
When we feel good emotions, there are benefits to our actions, so we are more compelled to commit to them.

Here's an example of something that could be beneficial, but currently isn't:

I want to lose a bit of weight and get in shape. It'll take some time, but I'll go to the gym, work out, and make it happen. I am going to figure out some way to find the time — regardless. And I am going to start planning ahead and making my own meals. Maybe I'll even check out one of those weight-loss services, which has everything set up for you. I just need to follow what they say. Then I'll wait, and my goal will be achieved.

Then you wait, wishing the entire time that you could stop thinking about all your favorite foods that you've been denying yourself. So you compromise, and decide that food will be your reward when you reach your goals for fitness and weight loss.

Maybe you are successful with this approach, maybe not. The big question is: Have you created new ways of thinking and responding that help you create a new way of living? Do you have a new mindset for success? Likely not (at least not for the long-term).

Now imagine what it'd be like to state your goal this way:

I'm so excited to be on my journey to lose some weight. I've had enough of being winded when I have to run upstairs. My pants are tight, and I'm just not as energetic as I used to be or want to be. If I can do this one thing, it will make it easier for everything else to fall into place.

Instead of spending a half-hour on Facebook, I'm going to start walking. Or maybe I'll do yoga. Exercise always feels so good. Not only will that feeling help me with my goals, it'll also make me feel better all-around.

No excuses!

Motivation is important. So take a few minutes to document how you feel about this journey.

_____

_____

_____

_____

Are your words and thoughts filled with excitement? Hopefully they are. If they aren't, rewrite your thoughts by using positive, inspirational wording.

_____

_____

_____

_____

What are three benefits you're going to receive by reconnecting with your intuition?

1. _____
2. _____
3. _____

Congratulations on completing the first step: Acknowledgment. It's exciting that you've achieved this building block! It will be the foundation of the next chapter, which is focused on taking action.

CHAPTER THREE

All Things Are Possible Through Action

There are many types of actions in our lives. Depending on our emotions, our frustrations, or the situations right in front of us, we may choose to act without even thinking twice about it; it just happens. Or maybe it's time to just do it, and I'm not referring to purchasing Nikes!

The three types of action that you need to be aware of are spontaneous action, anticipated action, and delayed action. The types of action we take are important, and we need to recognize the place we're taking action from. Is it fear? Are we passive? Or are we active in our pursuits?

Here's a brief overview of each of the three types of action:

- ✓ Spontaneous Action: Sometimes we need to take this kind of action. For instance, we may have to prevent a car accident or deal with an emergency. Spontaneous action is rooted in — and guided by — intuition. We know what to do, and we do not hesitate, ignore the situation, or second-guess ourselves. Our actions come from an "active" place.

- ✓ Anticipated Action: We want to do something, but only after we meet a list of certain criteria. For example, you state that you are going to take your dream vacation when you save up a certain amount of money. Or that you'll start a family after you've purchased a home. Intuition doesn't factor into anticipated action; it comes from a "passive" place.

- ✓ Delayed Action: This kind of action is a really nice term for procrastination and stagnancy. It's never beneficial. It does nothing to propel you forward, or help you recognize what you want. You spend a lot of time wishing for something, or maybe even feeling slighted about not having it. And it would have been quicker to just take the action, which comes from a place of fear.

We all take action in different ways. Ask yourself the following:

- ✓ What motivates you to take action?
- ✓ What fears do you have about taking action?
- ✓ Have you ever wished you acted on something, but you missed the right moment?
- ✓ Have you ever acted on something, only to learn that you should have been more patient?

Our intuition's innate wisdom works for us when we decide to take action, which includes passing up opportunities that outwardly seem decent, because something internally hinders us. Likewise, it also includes taking action that our outward thinking may be leery of. Perhaps we're afraid, or just resistant. Either way, if we want to reach our most amazing potential, we can't afford to *not* work with our intuition's guidance.

Now I want to share a great parable, which really shows the power of action in a meaningful way.

One day, a man was walking through the jungle, seeking some food. He was starving and couldn't find work. He happened to come upon a crippled pig, hobbling about noisily. He wondered how such an animal could feed itself. However, he was startled out of this thought when he saw a tiger stalking through the bushes, its captured prey dangling from its mouth. The tiger sat down on the ground and ate its fill. Then it got up and walked away, leaving the half-eaten carcass behind. After the tiger left, the pig made its way over, and began feasting on the remainder.

This situation was quite fascinating to the man. A marvelous thought came to him: *If the world can provide for that pig to eat, then it will provide for me, too.* This thought comforted him, and he headed back to his hut in a village at the edge of the jungle. When his time came, he would be prepared.

Much to his surprise, the shining image of a woman appeared before him and asked, "Why were you inspired by the crippled pig?"

"The world offered him the food he needed," the man said, his voice revealing his surprise about the vision.

"Don't you have gifts that contribute to the world, and could help you make a living? Why look to the crippled for inspiration, when you can follow the tiger, and provide for yourself *and* the crippled? Now get up and move."

The man was inspired into action by this visit. He saw that his results were the products of his own actions. From that day on, he vowed to no longer be the crippled pig, but to be the mighty tiger.

Do you take action to achieve, or wait to be served?

This chapter will walk you through your emotions and decisions regarding action. We'll start with fear, then move on to passivity, and finish with activity. You'll discover that you have a little bit of all of these types of action within you, due to your habits or desires (or the things you avoid). The goal is to be aware of *why* you are choosing to take action or remain inactive.

Fear-Driven Inactivity

Many adults think of Dr. Seuss as a quirky author who really excelled at giving kids great messages in an entertaining way. His books do that, of course, but the stories' lessons are meant for people of all ages. And in my best Seuss, I say, "If you live in fear, it will grind your gear, making it so you cannot steer." Hey, it's not quite Seussian, but you get the picture.

Fear is inexplicably crippling. Many times, we don't even realize how much it impacts us. Our relationships might not be as nourishing and loving as they could be, or our work might not be as rewarding or fulfilling as we want it to be. In general, if our minds are laced with doubt, the life we lead won't reach its maximum potential. Then all our energy is taken up by avoiding chances and distrusting our intuition.

Take a look at these statistics on fear.[4] They demonstrate this point perfectly:

- ✓ Let's start with a big one: 60% of the time, the things we fear never happen. That's more than half of our lives spent fearing something that won't occur. So that time spent afraid isn't productive, and it's certainly not intuitive.
- ✓ And how about this? About 30% of people waste time fearing what has already happened — instead of moving on, and feeling smarter and more aware. Trust yourself, learn, and grow!
- ✓ This one is the real kicker: 90% of what we fear is "insignificant." No, that's not a typo; it's insignificant. What does that tell you? Stop blowing things out of proportion!
- ✓ Many people worry about potential health issues, due to media hype or the ability to easily create a self-diagnosis. But nearly 88% of the time, these issues don't happen.
- ✓ In addition, approximately 6.3 million Americans have a phobia of some sort, with public speaking coming in at #1 (74%), death at #2 (68%), and spiders at #3 (30.5%).

But the great news is that fears can be overcome, and the exercise at the end of this chapter will help you do exactly that. Liberate yourself from fear. Embrace being bold!

---

[4] "Fear/Phobia Statistics." *Statistic Brain*. September 4, 2016. http://www.statisticbrain.com/fear-phobia-statistics/.

The Passivity Parade

It's charming to think we will have great lives if we just follow the Basic Rules of Humanity: Treat each other well, do the best you can at work, and make sure you're a responsible person. If you think that way, you might be one of the entries in the passivity parade.

Yes, it's nice to follow the Basic Rules of Humanity. Actually, they're essential for balance and harmony. However, there is so much more to life than rules. Let me ask you this: How can you reach your full potential if you're not linked to your instincts? How do you know — without a doubt — that you've received every opportunity that was designed for you?

You cannot guarantee you've achieved every opportunity if you're just doing what you have to do. In other words, you're being passive. Waiting and hoping are not beneficial uses of your time. Just believing something will happen is not enough. You must be committed to adjusting your intuition and instincts, so that you can be guided by something greater than mere acceptance.

If you're wondering if you're passive, ask yourself this question: Do people see you as someone un-invested in your life's outcome? And more importantly, do you see yourself that way?

My advice to everyone who has marched in the passivity parade:

Forgive yourself, and become an activist for your own wellbeing.

The benefits of transitioning from passivity to action are immense, and they'll help you redefine how you do everything in life — in the most incredible way possible. You will begin to do the following:

- ✓ Recognize what's important in life.
- ✓ Relax more.
- ✓ Reconsider your destiny.

For any person, those are three very important R's!

Thoughts, Ideas, and Actions

If you think you need a kick in the ass, here's an idea for you to consider: You probably do! And that's okay. Everyone has needed one at some point in their lives — including those who have experienced many successes, and have used many aspects of the 3 Second Rule.

I want to share something really interesting with you: A guy worked his way from thoughts to ideas, and then to actions. We'll call him Sam.

It begins with a simple series of realizations:

- ✓ Thoughts are what we believe internally.
- ✓ Ideas can challenge those thoughts, making us reconsider what we want to do in the future.

✓ Action is the way our thoughts and ideas come together. They are how we choose exactly what we are going to do.

Sam says he wants to keep the peace, but internalizing everything eats him up and stops him from realizing his full potential. There are times, though, when Sam gets tired and fed up with what's going on around him. Strong, random thoughts pop into his mind, such as: *I should really find a different group of friends;* or *I'd like to say something, but I won't;* or *If everyone just relaxed, things would be a whole lot better.*

Sam could act on any of these ideas. There is no reason why he couldn't find a new circle of friends. When others state their feelings, Sam is always welcome to do the same. In fact, he might be the one who says what everyone is already thinking. And as far as wishing everyone else would just relax, Sam might not be able to make it happen, but he can lead by example, can't he?

If Sam acted on any one of these ideas, he would experience an instant shift in his life. To be blunt, it might be as simple as shutting someone up who's nagging or whining. But it might actually be good to do that, and it would help him out as well.

How about you?

Are you an advocate for change in your own life? Keep in mind that it doesn't matter if you're right or wrong all of the time. Change requires action, and action can be linked to risk. However, the risk is reduced when you're linked to your intuition and allow it to act on your behalf.

Think of your own life as a corporation or organization. The same statistics on creating effective change apply in both scenarios. Now consider this:

70% of all changes attempted in an organization fail.[5]

Failure leads to debilitating emotions and thought patterns, which likely include fear about your career, concern for your family, and anxiety about your future. It's only when you can determine what causes failure that you can start to take action that works.

There are four main problems that result in an unsuccessful action. Let's consider each one for a moment.

1. Lack of knowledge
   An idea for change often cannot be executed without learning something first. For example, by reading this book, you're gaining an understanding of the process of intuition and the 3 Second Rule, which lays the groundwork for meaningful change.

---

[5] Why 70% of Changes Fail? Maurer, Rick. Online Magazine for Organizational Change Practitioners. September 19, 2010. http://www.reply-mc.com/2010/09/19/why-70-of-changes-fail-by-rick-maurer.

2. Lack of skill and practice

    Mastering our minds, bodies, and desires takes
    time and commitment. It's not something that
    happens overnight. Rather, it requires a plan of
    action and a genuine desire for change. Did you
    know that it's a myth that you can create a habit
    in 21 days? In the 1960s, a plastic surgeon named
    Maxwell Malts wrote a book called *Psycho-
    Cybernetics*. Based on how long it took his
    patients to get used to their new faces, it
    originated this myth: It takes 21 days to break a
    habit. In reality, research shows that it may take
    anywhere from 18 to 254 days to break a habit.[6]
    Determining factors include commitment to
    breaking the habit, how long the habit has existed
    (for example, how long you've smoked), and what
    the habit is. Some habits are harder to break than
    others. I don't know how disconnected you are
    from your intuition, but it's not easy to break the
    habit of listening to the conscious mind over
    your subconscious instinct. Be patient, but be
    disciplined.

3. Hidden and unresolved conflicts

    In order to take action that creates significant,
    positive change in your life, you have to address
    what you've left unattended in your emotional

[6] "Here's how long it takes to break a habit, according to science." Signe, Dean.
September 24, 2015. http://www.sciencealert.com/here-s-how-long-it-takes-to-
break-a-habit-according-to-science.

garden. Holding onto grudges and resentment weighs you down and makes listening to your intuition harder. In addition, not forgiving others stops you from forgiving yourself for your own situation. Call it "ditching your emotional baggage" or "cleaning up the house of your mind." But please do something, so you can experience greater things in life. Even a small grudge can slowly fester and get bigger over time.

4. Fear of change itself

    In the workplace, your coworkers' amassed fear can stifle change. But in your own life, you are solely responsible for stopping the fear of change from taking over. The simplest way to stop fear? Acknowledge it, and come up with the thoughts and ideas to overcome it. There's no greater way to accomplish this goal than creating a Personal Call to Action, which you'll learn how to do shortly.

Remember that every waking millisecond of every day in your life gives you a chance to take action.

Creating a Personal Call to Action (PCTA)

In marketing, a call to action is a way to provoke an immediate response from a target audience. Maybe it's as simple as telling them to "act now." But whatever it is, there's something that you're trying to compel them to do.

The definition of a PCTA is the following:

Finding the trigger that compels you to take immediate action in your personal life and strengthens your intuition.

Now I'm going to walk you through how to create a PCTA. This action will help you become the navigator of your own outcomes. It's based on what you want, as well as what you feel. The call to action can be as short as two words *if* you can remind yourself why your actions are important in two words. When creating your call to action, be careful and mindful, but also remember that no one knows how to do it better than you!

Case Study for a PCTA

Sheri is a 50-year-old account representative. She's done the job wonderfully for ten years, but she's ready to move on. And she's tried, but it hasn't worked out for her. Here's an example that shows her thought process at the current time.

Sheri sits up late at night, looking online at various opportunities for that "next step." She often finds positions that are interesting to her: They demand her skill set, and also offer the new challenges or experiences she craves. She yawns, thinking, "I'll do this first thing tomorrow morning." She goes to bed and thinks about the job, feeling excited about its potential. Eventually, she drifts off to sleep. Then tomorrow arrives, and she's immediately hurried and busy. Things get out of hand at work, and she gets home late, feeling wiped out. That interesting opportunity isn't even on her mind. Now she's just thinking about the weekend. And when the weekend comes, she's excited. She grabs her computer and goes to the jobsite where she saved the posting. Her heart sinks. It's no longer there. Job filled!

What could Sheri have done differently? Let's think... she could have:

- ✓ Applied for the job right when she saw it.
- ✓ Recognized that her busy, never-go-as-they're-planned weeks mean that she doesn't have the luxury of getting back to things the next day.
- ✓ Gotten out of bed to complete the application process after she recognized that she couldn't fall asleep because she was so excited.

But she did none of those things. Energy wasted. Stuck in her same routine. The potential of that opportunity is just gone.

Now let's walk Sheri through the ways she could have used a PCTA to help her out. Please remember that there are no wrong answers. The purpose is to give honest answers.

The first question for Sheri:
Why do you want to find a new job?

Her answer: I have worked hard and developed my skills. So now it is time to create a new challenge that will increase my income and be a good move for me.

The second question for Sheri:
What has stopped you from getting these opportunities in the past?
Her answer: A variety of things. One time, I was overqualified. Another time, I turned down an opportunity. But more often than not, I'm just too late by the time I show my interest.

The third question for Sheri:
Do you feel you deserve a new opportunity because you've demonstrated that you have what it takes?
Her answer: Yes, I work hard. It's just that I'm so tired at the end of the day, I only want to relax.

The fourth and last question for Sheri:
How much of a priority is a new job in your life?
Her answer: My top priority is paying off my credit card, which got a little out of control last year. But a new job is a solid second.

Now we know four things about Sheri. That's all we need to create her PCTA for finding a new career. A PCTA must do three things:

✓ Inspire
✓ Remind
✓ Compel

Sheri hears about the PCTA, and now she's excited and willing to give it a try. She's sick of missing out and tired of being tired (like so many people are). She starts to come up with a few ideas that might work:

✓ *Do it now.*
✓ *It might be gone tomorrow.* (Most PCTAs are positive, but negative motivators can work as well.)
✓ *This is my here and now.*
✓ *Opportunity breeds new energy.*

She thinks about these options for a day or two, and decides to go with: *This is my here and now.*

Then she gets back to work. Soon, she's on her computer at night again, surfing jobsites for that new chance. But because fate works in mysterious ways, she doesn't see a thing. Not that night. Not for two weeks. But she's diligent, and takes time to look each night. Finally, 16 days later, she sees an opportunity that interests her. It's almost 11 PM, and she has to get up at 6 AM to drive to a meeting a few hours away. But she remembers: *This is my here and now.* So she commits the same hour that she would have laid in bed thinking about it to completing a killer online application. Then she goes to bed, feeling accomplished and peaceful. The next day, on her way back from that meeting, she gets a call: "Hi Sheri, we'd like to talk with you about your application. When are you available?"

What a difference a thought makes. Don't ever let anyone tell you differently.

PCTAs can be created for any area of your life that you seek change in, including reconnecting with your intuition.

Activating Your Action

What do I fear? What am I passive about? Why do I take action? The answers to these three questions will create the second important building block in the bridge between your life and your intuition.

In this section, we are going to address the things you fear, which are actually opportunities that are usually missed. Then we will leverage your fears or completely eradicate them. It's important to know what your current tendencies are. Think of yourself as a tough cowboy, and wrangle up anything that doesn't bring you fulfillment. Once you know what actions to take, the potentials are endless.

What Do I Fear?

Reflect on the following questions about fear. Your fears may be about your own life, or they may be about others. Either way, your perception impacts you.

- ✓ Have you sensed that fear holds you back in certain situations?

- ✓ When you think about your fears, are you more afraid of failure, physical harm, or emotional harm? Perhaps all three?
- ✓ Is your fear based on what you cannot control, or how others will respond to your actions?
- ✓ What types of experiences have you had in the past that increased your fear?
- ✓ Do you *consciously* know when you're fearful?
- ✓ What do you fear more: Something bad happening to you, or the emotional repercussions of it? (For example: You invest your last $100 in hopes of making $200. But you end up with nothing, and beat yourself up over it.)

Do the people around you add to your fear, or detract from it?

_____

Regarding your fear, how do you feel about the messaging of your internal dialogue?

_____
_____
_____

What are three things about your fears that you would like to shift to a more positive mindset?

_____
_____
_____

You know yourself best. What would make you commit to lessening fear and emboldening your intuition *if* you really wanted to? And I believe you do! What are three things that you can do to begin this process?

_____

_____

_____

Now it's time to offer you a few suggestions for positive affirmations regarding fear. Remember to refer to Appendix A for tips and wisdom about using affirmations.

Also remember that affirmations are precise, positive, and easy to remember. Here are some wonderful choices about conquering fear:

- ✓ I will stare anything in the eye.
- ✓ I've got this!
- ✓ I choose positive directives to guide me.
- ✓ My destiny is in my hands.
- ✓ I trust myself.

Choose an affirmation that resonates with you, or create your own. Just remember to keep it positive. And take action! This choice isn't on your to-do list; it's on your must-do-always list.

What Am I Passive About?

Being passive doesn't mean that you don't care. It means you let everyone else dictate your outcome. It's one of the most detrimental things you can do, as it rapidly severs you from your intuition. When you're passive, these are the messages you're sending to other people:

- ✓ You don't care.
- ✓ You will just do whatever.
- ✓ You are lazy.
- ✓ You don't have a clue.

Dang! For most people, none of those things are true, but people treat others the way they perceive them. Do you think that someone would walk up to Bill Gates or Meg Whitman and respond to them as if they were passive? No, never. Why? Because people like Gates and Whitman understand that their actions don't dictate their opportunities. They also know that their actions dictate how people respond to them, and they exude confidence about their decisions and abilities. People such as Gates and Whitman are connected to their intuition, which shows without them having to say a word. You don't have to be bold and loud to be active. You just have to be aware of your own value.

Think about how others perceive you based on your actions. Write these perceptions down:

_____

_____

Do you like or dislike these perceptions? Why?

_____

_____

Do you want to change these perceptions?

1. Yes
2. No

Why or why not?

_____

_____

What is one thing you can do today to become less passive?

_____

_____

When you reflect on how you answered these questions, did you find that you were aware of what you were passive about, or did you have to think about it? If you were aware of it, you have an edge: You are already somewhat intuitive about your passivity. Being aware is part of the battle. But it's not most of the battle. I'd be doing you a disservice if I said it was. The biggest battle (and eventual victory) will occur when you start taking action.

Why Do I Take Action?

The meaning of the word "action" depends on the situation. It can have one of these three meanings:

1. *The fact or process of doing something, typically to achieve an aim.* For example, she was committed to changing her actions that were rooted in fear.

2. *Something you do.* For example, he often questioned the actions he took.

3. *The manner or style of doing something, typically the way in which a mechanism works or a person moves.* For example, I'm starting to understand my mind's actions when I'm stressed out.

Knowing how and why we act is where it all starts. All three meanings come into play in our lives, which means that it's important for us to consider action in every sense of the word.

Here's the question you should really weigh when you're thinking about the actions you take: What's driving the action?

The next essential step is finding how to motivate yourself to take action. It's also a strong step toward further connecting yourself to your intuition. In what ways could you motivate yourself to take action, when you were once fearful or passive? Remember, small steps can lead to big strides, and they help build the bridge to your intuition. Be excited about being fearless.

_____

_____

_____

_____

What are realistic timelines to attain your goals of becoming fearless? Pick one area that you want to focus on first, and document how the process will work for you. Take note: That's "will work," not "might work!"

_____
_____
_____
_____

What are three benefits that you're going to receive by focusing on taking action as a way to reconnect with your intuition?

1. _____
2. _____
3. _____

Congratulations on completing the second action step. The foundation of another exciting building block has been laid! What's next? It's time to focus on your self-awareness.

"Action is the foundational key to all success."
~Pablo Picasso~

CHAPTER FOUR

Self-Awareness

Our self-awareness is like the leader of all our emotional faculties. It helps us determine how we're acting, and why. Let's face it: Sometimes, we have strange, unexpected responses, often without having any consciously known rhyme or reason. When we become self-aware, we are better able to process the following:

- ✓ Change
- ✓ Desire
- ✓ Reason
- ✓ Logic
- ✓ Motivation

How confident are you about understanding how every action you take impacts your goals, whether large or small? Growing more self-aware requires answering that question.

Has the following situation ever happened to you?

You're feeling off one day. You're lost in thought. You're griping about what isn't happening, and all the things that you don't feel that you're in control of. Of course, you're at work when all this is going on, so you feel trapped and eager for the day to be done. Then you can go home and wallow in your glum mood by yourself. You feel so bad that even your misery doesn't want company.

A peer comes up to you with a package he was told to deliver. "Here you go," he says. You look at him, and laser beams of discontent shoot out of your eyes. He takes a protective step backward. Frowning, you ask him directly, "What is it?" He replies, "I was told to give it to you."

You frown again and look at the package. Your peer is still there, not really sure what to do. Then you grit your teeth. Why are you getting this package back again? You sent it out twice already. Now what's wrong? Then your filter clogs up, and you begin to speak bluntly and angrily: "This is ridiculous. If he doesn't like it, he should fix it himself."

Meanwhile, this person is looking at you, and all he can say is, "Sorry, I was just asked to bring it to you." Then he turns around and runs away from you like he's Usain Bolt. And believe me, he's really sorry about being in the wrong place at the wrong time. Suddenly, you're really embarrassed. Now you have to deliver a genuine apology, because you know that you acted through some channel of anger that isn't authentic.

But... you have to let go. And grow.

How do you do that?

You move on by making the entire experience a lesson in self-awareness, and you find a way to trigger a smarter strategy to master your days, even when you're in a bad mood.

According to an article by Anthony K. Tjan, "Without self-awareness, you cannot understand your strengths and weakness, your 'superpowers' versus your 'kryptonite.' It is self-awareness that allows the best business-builders to walk the tightrope of leadership: projecting conviction while simultaneously remaining humble enough to be open to new ideas and opposing opinions. The conviction (and yes, often ego) that founders and CEOs need to fulfill their vision makes them less than optimally wired for embracing vulnerabilities or leading with humility. All this makes self-awareness that much more essential." [7]

While this statement is about business, it is easy to see how these same principles apply to our personal lives as well. There really is no separation between business life and private life. If you are being truthful, you know that you can't simply forget work the minute you walk out of the office for the day. However, if you know how to grow in business, you can grow in your personal life as well. Likewise, personal growth is often accompanied by professional growth.

There are three ways to ensure that we are becoming more self-aware. They involve building and acknowledging the need for confidence, understanding, and goal-setting.

These three strategies are loosely based on the sentiment that Tjan shared in his article. They are:

1. **Know yourself better by testing yourself.**

   There are a number of personality tests out there. Are they always 100% accurate? No, but they are almost always insightful. Plus, they get you thinking about what type of person you are — just like this book is doing.

---

[7] How Leaders Become Self-Aware. Tjan, Anthony K. Harvard Business Review. July 19, 2012. https://hbr.org/2012/07/how-leaders-become-self-aware.html.

2. **Watch yourself and learn.**

    No matter how busy or self-absorbed most people are, you're probably still aware of your actions and their repercussions. Maybe you're in line behind a slow person, and instead of being angry about it, you decide to breathe in and check your social media. When you finally check out and leave, you see that there's an accident up ahead, which you could have been in. In that moment, you're grateful to have a moment of clarity. The key is to carry that moment of clarity into all areas of your life. Embrace that things are sometimes not going to happen when you want them to, but you can always keep learning, growing, and moving forward.

3. **Be aware of others.**

    Sources of inspiration are all around us. For instance, maybe you always get stuck writing the introduction to a report at work. There's probably someone who can easily write that introduction, and is glad to help. Or maybe you want to get a doggie portrait taken as a surprise for your wife. You know that someone in accounting did that for her husband, so you ask her about it. Everyone around you can be a resource for personal growth. You should be thankful. Also, you should strive to be that type of person for others. Self-awareness can help you in all areas of your life!

When you know yourself, you can then focus on improving yourself, which is the gift of self-awareness. And no other activity can replicate or replace it.

The Confidence Cog

Our confidence is influenced by a wide variety of factors in our lives. Here are some of the most common factors that impact our level of confidence:

- ✓ Physical health concerns
- ✓ A perceived lack of self-control
- ✓ Frustrating and adverse relationships in our personal lives
- ✓ Volatile relationships in our professional lives
- ✓ Traumatic experiences from childhood
- ✓ Poor or inept decision-making patterns

These types of events lessen our self-esteem, and therefore our confidence. First, I should clarify the difference between self-esteem and confidence, as these terms are often used interchangeably. Here's the definition of each, according to *Merriam-Webster's Online Dictionary*:

Self-esteem: A feeling of satisfaction that people have in themselves or their own abilities.

Confidence: Having a feeling or belief that you can do something well or succeed at something.

As you can see, self-esteem is what we build up, in order to give us confidence. You cannot have confidence without self-esteem, and vice-versa. Are there people who do wonderful things but lack confidence? Yes, but they don't acknowledge their successes, despite others complimenting them about them.

How about you? Do others give you compliments about your skills, gifts, and talents? If they do, think about your response. Hopefully, you don't discredit these compliments. But if you do, you have a self-esteem issue that you should start addressing.

Self-esteem is essential for creating a 3 Second Rule way of life, because it allows you to gain the confidence to start employing the Rule. Then you can create effective and meaningful changes in your life – every day, and in a fraction of the time that it currently takes you.

Here are a few things that you can do to help lift up your self-esteem:

✓ **Be nice to yourself.**
   Focus on having good hygiene habits. When we feel good, we are more likely to exude confidence and receive opportunities.
✓ **Manage your stress.**
   This goal can be accomplished by exercising, not being too hard on yourself, and not overbooking your schedule.
✓ **Get enough rest.**
   When we're tired, everything seems worse.

✓ **Do kind things for others.**

    Few things give us as much internal joy as helping others. Embrace this habit in some way, whether it's large or small.

How we view ourselves is a combination of what we personally do, and how those around us treat us. This concept should never be forgotten.

A Power Parable

There was a young woman who felt lost — like she was a failure. She wasn't as talented as her sister, nor as successful as her cousin. She just couldn't take it any longer. At her wit's end, she went to the local wise man in her small village.

"I'm so tired, sir. I just want to end it all. What can I do?"

"Go away," the man said. "I'm busy. Unless..." Then he offered to help her later, if she'd agree to help him at that moment. He gave her a precious red ruby, and told her to take it to the market and try to sell it. "But," the man said, "You should settle for no less than fifty gold coins."

She went to the market and went from person to person. Everyone said no to fifty gold coins, but some offered her fifteen or twenty. Feeling sad that she couldn't even complete that simple task, she dejectedly made her way back to the wise man, telling him how she'd failed.

The wise man considered this development. He recommended that she go to the local jeweler and see what he had to say. She agreed and went to the jewelry store. When she handed him the stone, he said, "This is worth at least seventy gold coins. I don't have all that money right now, but I shall soon."

The young woman breathed a sigh of relief, elated by what he had shared with her. She was very excited to report this news to the wise man. When she got there and told him the story, he smiled knowingly and said, "Remember, sweet girl, you are like this ruby: both precious and unique. Only a real expert can appreciate your true value. So why are you wasting your time by wandering through the market and heeding the opinions of fools?"

I love this parable. It perfectly encapsulates the point that we often put too much value on what others say, without regarding their motives or knowledge. If we undervalue ourselves, others will, too. But if we value ourselves, we will gain the confidence to seek out advisers whose opinions of us are meaningful and important.

Understanding Our Nuanced Motives

Frequently, the source of our motivation can also be the source of our problems. If we're motivated to be like the best version of someone else, we're not motivated by something that is really sustainable and meaningful to us. However, if we're motivated to be the best versions of our authentic selves, we are tapped into something that's really special and effective.

Daniel Pink, a known expert on motivation, wrote an excellent book called *Drive: The Surprising Truth About What Motivates Us*. In an interview that he did with Katherine Bell of The Harvard Business Review Ideacast, an interesting exchange occurred. Here's an excerpt from it.[8]

KATHERINE BELL: *So tell us, in a nutshell, what was most surprising that you found about what does motivate us?*

DANIEL PINK: *Well, I guess what surprised me the most was these kind of motivators that we take pretty much a given, that you know, if you reward something, you get more of that behavior, if you punish, you get less of it. That turns out to be not true in a surprisingly wide band of circumstances. These carrot and stick motivators, which are very, very good for certain things, actually aren't very good for many, if not most things. And a lot of the research that I looked at in this book- and to write it, I looked at about 40 or 50 years of research in behavioral science- it really overturned a lot of my own preset notions about why we do what we do.*

KATHERINE BELL: *So has what motivates people changed, or do we just understand more about human motivation after the last 40 years or so of research?*

---

[8] What Motivates Us? An interview with Katherine Bell and Daniel Pink. Harvard Business Review Ideacast. February 18, 2010.
https://hbr.org/2010/02/what-motivates-us.

DANIEL PINK: *You know what, I think it's a mix of both. That's a really, really interesting question. Human beings, by the nature of their being human beings, are a mix of drives. So we have a biological drive. We eat when we're hungry, we drink when thirsty. We have a reward and punishment drive, so we do respond very well to rewards and punishments in our environment. Then we have this third drive, that often gets neglected in business, where we do things because they're interesting, because they're fun, because we like them, because they contribute.*

Now, I can bet those three drives have always been what constitutes being a human being, and I don't think that people's motivations have changed significantly, say, over the last 40 or 50 years. I think what has changed are a couple of things. Number one is that there's now a very large body of research that gives us a much more calibrated, sophisticated understanding of how motivation works. The second thing is that, actually, I think what's changed is not the motivation, but the type of work that people are doing.

So these characteristic motivators, these if-then rewards, they're really good for simple, straightforward, rule-based, what we might think of as algorithmic tasks, where you're just following a set of instructions. And that's what a lot of Americans– a lot of people in the industrialized world– did for a living for very long time. I mean, a lot of work was about turning the same screw the same way over and over, and when that kind of work started fading away, a lot of work- a lot of white collar work- was in some ways simply adding up columns of figures over and over again. That is, it was intellectual work, but it was pretty routine, algorithmic kind of work.

And the truth is, what the science tells us is that for that kind of work, these carrot and stick, if-then motivators, they're pretty good. They work pretty well. They don't exactly ennoble the human spirit, but they're fairly effective. The trouble is, is that for work that is non-routine, for work that isn't algorithmic but is more conceptual, that requires big picture thinking, that requires a greater degree of creativity, that requires solving more complicated, complex challenges, the if-then motivators don't work very well at all. And that's not even a close call in the science. The behavioral science is very, very clear that- give people those kinds of motivators for creative, conceptual, complex tasks, and they will often underperform.

So I think that people have always had this mix of drives, that's what it is to be human, so I don't think that their motivations necessarily have changed. I think what's changed though, is the work that people are doing requires in some ways, a different technology for motivating people to do it.

***

In order to be motivated, we first have to be more self-aware about what we want. Many people are motivated by something negative that happened to them. Unlike many, I don't think that's necessarily bad, as long as you use it to do something good.

Here's a great example: I heard about a guy who was really heavy in high school, and got married right after graduation. But eventually, his wife became really turned off by his weight and left him for a "buffer model." He was emotionally crushed, and his confidence was at an all-time low. But then he thought, *I want to show that I'm just as good, if not better, than the guy she left me for.* Not a positive motivator by most standards. However, he used this concept to create a disciplined habit to exercise more, eat better, and put himself out there to show that he's of value. And it all worked and proved his value. Why? He believed in the results, so they started to happen. He could have even gotten the girl back, but he passed. Instead, he got a new job, a new perspective, and a new habit of taking care of himself that served him well. (Remember the previous pointers about self-esteem.)

Mission accomplished.

What motivates you more than anything? Here are some of the most positive motivators:

- ✓ Self-improvement
- ✓ Better things for your life, and your family's lives
- ✓ A feeling of accomplishment
- ✓ Continual growth with no stagnancy

✓ And fun! It's indeed fun to achieve and experience improvements in your life

Through motivation, we can set strong goals that keep us moving forward.

Creating Stronger Goals Through Self-Awareness

For most people, goals are both an overused and under-utilized word. I'm no different. I've made goals and abandoned them, but I've also made goals and been inspired by them. And I'm determined to succeed no matter what. It all depends on — you guessed it — my actual desire to achieve the goal.

I recently heard something else that really resonates with me. It's a different approach to goals, and I find it very helpful. Maybe it'll work for you if you've been through one of these wringers: Setting the wrong goals, setting goals that could not be achieved, or abandoning goals when you're even slightly distracted. Here's what I've heard:

If you've achieved a goal, you haven't set your sights high enough.

Why do I like this statement?

Because it reminds me of the bridge we're building as we learn the 3 Second Rule. Think of a goal as a step on the staircase to success. You know what you have to do next, and you have an idea about where you're going. But you give yourself the flexibility to adapt the following truisms as you see fit:

- Life changes
- Goals change
- Needs change

Therefore, our goals have to be flexible enough to change as well, but only if we understand why we're changing them. We can't use their flexibility as an excuse for not doing our due diligence. And, regarding the development of intuition, it definitely takes intentional due diligence to get to a place where your intuition is working for you without consciously intending to.

The following three factors are vital to the success or failure of a goal of any size:

- ✓ Not having a plan
- ✓ Only planning in your head
- ✓ Writing the plan down

When we are mindful of this concept, we can set S.M.A.R.T.E.R. goals: [9]

S: Specific
Vague goals cannot motivate you or help you lay out a meaningful direction. For example, being happier

---

[9]Setting S.M.A.R.T.E.R. Goals: 7 Steps to Achieving Any Goal. Wanderlust Worker. 2016. https://www.wanderlustworker.com/setting-s-m-a-r-t-e-r-goals-7-steps-to-achieving-any-goal/.

tomorrow has no value, although it sounds nice. You have to phrase it like this: I am going to do *xyz* today because it will make me happier tomorrow.

M: Meaningful
If a goal is not truly meaningful to you, its chances of failure significantly increase.

A: Achievable
Having goals that force you out of your comfort zone is great, but they have to be achievable. For example, you cannot become a pilot in a few days, or lose fifty pounds in a month.

R: Relevant
It's important to set goals that serve a genuine purpose and are relevant to your life. For example, you will likely abandon a goal to raise money for a cause you don't really participate in.

T: Time-bound
A goal with no end in sight is not a goal, just a pipedream. Set goals for various dates (such as one day, week, month, or year from now), and create strategies to maintain regular forward progress regarding these goals.

E: Evaluate
Set measures by which you can clearly tell if you are making headway toward your goals. Without them, you can only speculate, which is seldom favorable.

R: Readjust

Based on your results for a S.M.A.R.T.E.R goal, you will be able to determine how to readjust. Are you where you thought you'd be? Is your goal still meaningful? What did you learn that might impact that?

By being smart about goals, you can be motivated to achieve them, and it can be fun. Truly rewarding, actually.

Activating Your Self-Awareness

Every step, strategy, and concept in this book is a game-changer. But answering the three questions above make up the third block of the bridge you're building to intuition: Gaining confidence, understanding yourself, and achieving goals. But from personal experience (as well as what I've witnessed in others), let me tell you that confidence and self-awareness are game-changers. Things happen when we're confident and self-aware. We flourish!

How do you increase confidence, understand yourself more fully, and begin achieving your goals? It's important to know what your tendencies are at this moment in your life. It doesn't matter who you are at this moment, where you've been, or even where you want to go. But here's what does matter: You should approach things from the proper mindset and perspective.

Gaining Confidence

Before this section begins, it's important to note the following: Overconfidence is often a sign that someone is compensating for a lack of confidence. It's like smoke and mirrors — out there to deceive and protect the person who's struggling. Are you coping with confidence issues? If so, accept the truth of it, and know that you won't be judged here.

To gauge where you stand with respect to your confidence, take a look at these questions:

✓ Have you ever done anything to increase your self-confidence, such as take a course, read a book, or seek hypnosis or therapy? How did you feel about the results? If someone criticizes you, whether crudely or constructively, are you able to listen and separate your emotions from what they're sharing?

✓ If you feel that you're being treated unjustly in a work situation, can you comfortably address the person who's the source of the problem?

✓ When you feel that you're being taken advantage of in your personal life, are you able to explain what you're feeling? In other words, are you able to stick to that specific topic, and nothing else?

✓ Do you feel that shy people can be confident? Why or why not?

✓ When you're uncertain about a situation, do you try to "fake it till you make it," or do you try a different tactic? Maybe admit that you are unsure, and share what you know? Or something else?

- ✓ If you see a beautiful person, do you have the ability to go up to them and tell them so (no strings attached, just a simple compliment)?
- ✓ Are you aware of the areas of your life that you're most confident in?

Do you feel like you solely control your level of confidence?

Based on how you felt about these questions, what are your thoughts about your confidence level?

_____

_____

_____

Regarding confidence, how do you feel about the messaging of your internal dialogue?

_____

_____

_____

What are three benefits that excite you about gaining confidence?

1. _____
2. _____
3. _____

What are your thoughts about your self-esteem? Do you think that it hinders you from being more confident, and experiencing a better quality of life?

_____

_____

Now it's time to offer you a few suggestions for positive affirmations about building self-esteem and confidence. This concept is really important, because all growth in your life is linked to these two factors.

Here are some wonderful "I statements" for increasing self-esteem and confidence levels:

- ✓ I am a person of value.
- ✓ I grow stronger and better every day.
- ✓ I am the one who determines my outcome.
- ✓ I want to be more confident, and that is a good thing.
- ✓ I know that I'm a valuable person.

As always, start with one of these tactics to help you out, or create your own. Do whatever you have to do to include them in your routine. You could even do online research. Remember, Appendix A explains all the ways you can use affirmations in your life.

Understanding Yourself

Many of us have thought or spoken, "No one gets me!" But we seldom think about ourselves. Do we understand ourselves? Can you always explain why you feel a certain way? Probably not. No one can all the time. However, if we understand ourselves better, all the dwelling and debating lessens as our self-awareness rises. Intuitive answers instantly start kicking in. In other words, they occur in less than 3 seconds!

How do you know if you understand yourself? Consider these generalized statements:

- ✓ You get flustered or change the subject if someone asks you to clarify your opinion.
- ✓ You often struggle to make up your mind.
- ✓ You choose to focus on taking care of everyone else, instead of yourself.
- ✓ You remain quiet, rather than starting a conversation that you don't know how to finish.
- ✓ When you think about having quiet time, you'd rather put your head between two clashing symbols than dare going into "unknown territory."

You're brave and strong. You've got this! You can learn to understand yourself better. In fact, it's quite a relief to really know yourself. The times when I've felt like I was acting against my best interests — or was so busy that I couldn't focus on them — were always the toughest, least rewarding times in my life. Not to be cliché, but I lost myself. Thankfully, we can all be found again (without an entire search party) by giving ourselves some much needed "me time." Use that time to figure things out, and start living a life that's power-driven by self-understanding.

Think about how you gauge your self-awareness. Do you understand your own actions? If you do (or don't), how do you know?

_____

_____

Pretend you're a teacher. Give yourself a grade, in order to understand what drives you. What explanation would you attach to that grade?

_____

_____

Are you willing to commit to steps and strategies, in order to understand yourself better?
1. Yes
2. No

How do you see this situation benefiting you?

_____

_____

What is one thing you can do today that will help you more fully understand how to respond to a situation that's weighing you down?

_____

_____

When you reflect on your answers, were you surprised that you didn't understand your actions, motives, and activities as well as you thought? The exciting news is that once you begin using the 3 Second Rule, you won't have to consciously think about understanding yourself. Your intuition gets it. No explanations needed. It just knows what to do. And, if it does falter, it won't be nearly as bad as the ways that your conscious mind and ego have failed you in the past. Human beings make mistakes, even those with profound intuition.

Achieving Goals

Our goals are our directions toward knowing — without a doubt — that we have achieved something we set out to do. It's hard not to love that concept, and rally behind it!

We're going to have many goals throughout our lives. Some of them may be simultaneously worked on, while others replace goals that we abandon or don't accomplish. And as long as we maintain the proper mindset, we will keep growing. And it will be amazing.

I want you to focus on this goal right now: <u>I am going to enhance my intuition until I'm able to naturally live in a 3 Second Rule state of being</u>.

Now it's time to get S.M.A.R.T.E.R. about it as well. Your challenge is to go through this activity and create a customized intuition goal, based on your understanding of yourself. Are you ready?

S — Specific: I've got this one covered!
<u>I am going to enhance my intuition until I'm able to naturally live in a 3 Second Rule state of being</u>.

M – Meaningful: Why is this goal meaningful to you?

_____

_____

_____

_____

A – Achievable: How do you know you can accomplish this goal?

_____

_____

_____

_____

R – Relevant: What relevance does this goal have for you?

_____

_____

_____

_____

T – Time-bound: From this point on, how much time do you think you'll need to achieve a 3 Second Rule state of being?

_____

_____

_____

_____

E – Evaluate: How often do you take a look at your goal and its progress?

_____

_____

_____

_____

R — Readjust: How will you know it's time to adjust your goal, so you can succeed at it?

_____

_____

_____

_____

You've just done something huge. How do you feel about it?

_____

_____

_____

_____

At this moment, what do you think your chances are of accomplishing this goal? And why?

_____

_____

_____

_____

What are three benefits of using goals for this life-changing, positive purpose?

1. _____
2. _____
3. _____

Congratulations on completing the third step of self-awareness! Your bridge is coming along nicely, and it's about to expand even further as you dive into the next step: Desires.

CHAPTER FIVE

Desires

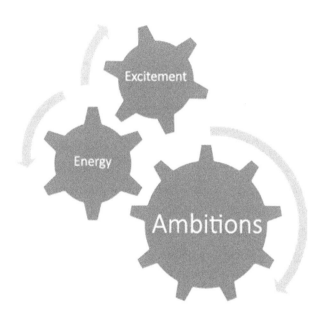

When you desire something, you cannot help but notice that desire. It frequently consumes your thoughts, daydreams, and conversations.

If your desire is to have a relationship, someone new may really capture your attention. You cannot stop thinking about him or her, and envisioning what some sort of future together might be like.

When you commit to making a change in your life, you feel this excited energy start surging through you. It expands your thoughts, and allows you to tap into all positive benefits that this change may offer. These kinds of feelings are particularly strong when it comes to a career shift, or even moving to a new place. After all, new places mean new beginnings. And new beginnings are exciting.

Of course, desiring these changes is only great if you decide to actually pursue the change. However, many times, these changes are only temporary. Sure, we may end up making more money, but in the end, we still have ourselves to deal with. And for some people, a job will always just be a job. Even with relationships, the "new relationship high" eventually wears off. Both of you will still have the habits you had prior to meeting, but now you're less likely to show your best side. So your real thoughts and feelings will come out. Maybe you'll remain compatible, or maybe you won't. Anyone who's tried to make it in the dating world has likely asked, "What happened to that person I met? He (or she) isn't the same anymore." Do these questions bring back any memories?

Our desires are very much like that "new relationship high." I define this feeling in the following way:

The energy you use to give your best effort, because you want it to work. It feels good, and it stimulates you in a positive, motivating way.

Change — sometimes, even a scary change — can bring about a "new relationship high." It excites us. It stirs up the pot, if you will. We force ourselves to think about something that isn't a part of our daily grind. And we desire because the object of our desire is new, and stops us from feeling bored or complacent.

How do you use this type of energy? And do you know how to harvest and sustain it?

Newsflash: Desire doesn't have to be a fleeting fancy or a temporary state of being. When you tap into your instincts, you start connecting with desires that match you perfectly — whether they're for your life, career, or something completely different. It's such a wonderful feeling. If you tap into your instincts in this way, you'll always have desires. And you'll maintain the passion to pursue them, so you'll put them in your "active column." It doesn't make sense to be passive about something that you say you want, that you feel you want, and that's great for you, does it?

The 3 Second Rule is based on rules that stem from your need for personal growth and fulfillment. The energy to pursue these kinds of desires is very significant, and it can take you quite far. If you don't utilize this energy, it will be nothing short of tragic. Think of the saddest story you've ever heard about someone who didn't achieve their potential, and lump it in with not acknowledging and pursuing your desire for personal betterment. Then you'll get the idea.

Here are some things that desires for personal growth allow you to do:

- ✓ Not invest your energy in stagnancy.
- ✓ Embrace change, even when it may be scary or really — and I mean really — outside of your comfort zone.
- ✓ Remain happy with your progress, even in those moments when it feels like the world is crumbling around you. You control your desires, not anyone else.
- ✓ Look at things from a kinder, less fearful perspective.
- ✓ Grant yourself permission to take calculated risks in your life.
- ✓ See how important and special other people's successes are.

So you have desire. What's next?

In this chapter, we're going to tap into how to respond to that excitement when we feel desire, find ways to sustain the energy that desire naturally promotes within us, and learn ways to hone in on ambitions that "keep the drive alive."

Feel the Excitement

Remember when you were a little kid, and you felt really excited about something? Maybe it was Christmas, your upcoming family vacation, the last day of school, or your birthday. You were on such a high that it was hard to focus on anything else, and all you wanted to do was live, breathe, and talk about what excited you. Then the event happened, and it was all you dreamed it would be. But then it was gone and done – your weeks' worth of excitement ended in a single day. It's a sensation similar to a sugar high wearing off: "The plunge."

After the plunge, you begin wondering and doubting. And it isn't very fun at all, in comparison to what you were previously so excited about.

You've probably had one of these thoughts:

- ✓ *Now what?*
- ✓ *Nah, that sounds dull.*
- ✓ *Darn, you mean I have to wait another year for my birthday?*

It's time to harness your excitement!

Would you be surprised to hear that excitement and anxiety are two sides of the same coin? It's true. According to Stephane Gaskin, PhD:

> **Anxiety** is a negative state of mind. It is characterized by heightened physiological arousal (such as faster

heartbeat and respiration), which is often accompanied by a sensation of dread. We often feel anxious and pressured about performing a task that involves an evaluation, since it involves an uncertain future.

Excitement is a positive state of mind. It is also associated with physiological arousal, which is the same feeling that you have when you experience anxiety. When we anticipate that an event will go well, we feel excited: It will bring us joy, and we will succeed.[10]

I have to wonder: Why is it that the excitement we feel as children often turns into the anxiety of adulthood? Suddenly, Christmases, vacations, and birthdays all become sources of anxiety. Why? We equate them with using up a lot of our "precious" time, and/or costing us money that we may not really have. As far as birthdays, we often feel like we haven't really hit our stride or reached our fullest potential. When we feel that way, birthdays suddenly become reminders of what we haven't done, and remind us that we have one year less to accomplish these goals.

Think of how awesome birthdays were for many of us when we were younger.

---

[10] Anxiety or Excitement: It's Up to You. Gaskin PhD, Stephane. Coaching S Gaskin Precision and Direction. January 24, 2014.
http://www.coachingsgaskin.com/anxiety-or-excitement-its-up-to-you/.

First, we got to turn 10. *Reaching double digits. Sweet!*

Then we turned 13. *Yes, finally a teenager. Now I'll be taken seriously!*

And 16. *Driving. Freedom!*

Wow, 18! *Welcome to the awesomeness of adulthood, and not having to follow everyone else's orders.*

Then 21. *Awesome! You can actually go to a bar and buy that beer.*

What happens next? Many people (and thankfully, this is starting to change) begin dreading their birthdays.

30 — *No way! My third decade of life. Ugh!*

40 — *Time is going by way too quickly.*

50 — *How did I become a half-century old? Where has the time gone?*

Then, if you're fortunate, you'll start believing that it's a pretty great miracle that you made it to retirement. Then you're 80, 90, etc.

Dang... Who wouldn't give anything to look forward to their birthday again? Your birthday used to be a sign of the great things to come, and a celebration of all the things you'd accomplished!

Today is your opportunity to channel that kid in you, who knew you'd experience some great things as time passed. Allow yourself to generate that excitement again. It will help build the bridge to living in the most authentic way — to living the 3 Second Rule way. Your intuition loves excitement, and knows how to continuously feed on it.

Then you can keep the excitement alive, and you'll attract the following:

- ✓ New opportunities
- ✓ Better opportunities
- ✓ The right opportunities

Likewise, your excited intuitive state will repel the following:

- ✓ Bad opportunities
- ✓ The wrong opportunities

And how exactly is an opportunity defined? According to the Cambridge English Dictionary, an opportunity is *an occasion or situation that makes it possible to do something that you want to do or have to do, or the possibility of doing something.* [11]

Knowing that opportunities and excitement are intricately linked, wouldn't it be great to know that you're giving yourself the right inner resources? That you're using your

---

[11] http://dictionary.cambridge.org/us/dictionary/english/opportunity.

intuition to maximize your potential? There's no better way to achieve this goal than expelling anxiety – and all the negativity associated with it – while maintaining excitement about all the wonderful desires it creates.

There are some pretty fantastic ways to create and maintain excitement. Consider trying one of these, or a number of them:

1. **Go to events that interest you.**
   A wonderful way to get excited is to participate in something that interests you. Some examples may be volunteer work for charities you support, political rallies, or church groups. They can help you meaningfully connect with your local community.

2. **Seek out new places to explore.**
   An experience that garners excitement doesn't have to come from an expensive vacation. It can also come from checking out something that just seems interesting. Have you ever read an ad or a sign, and wondered what a business was all about? Go find out! Some of the best surprises are close to home.

3. **Make time for "you time."**
   Don't discredit spending time alone. The benefits are vast. Alone time can create desires for things you've never even considered – or have long forgotten as you hustle through your days, too exhausted to even want to think at night.

According to Dr. Mercola, 85% of Americans think it's important to spend time completely alone.[12] So if you agree with the majority, the next step is to actually schedule some alone time.

4. <u>Save up for something you want.</u>
While material things can never create true happiness, they can offer energy and something to be excited about — particularly if what you want will help you work on you. Remember, you're someone that's worth working on! A friend of mine used this concept to save up and attend the seminars of some well-known thought leaders.

5. <u>Surprise someone.</u>
When we surprise someone, we tend to be as excited about what we're doing as the recipient of the surprise. It feels good to make others feel good.

6. <u>Spend quality time with someone.</u>
These moments are very exciting — whether they're dates with your partner or spouse, or going to see someone just to catch up. Quality time is also good for discovering positive activities, which are pathways that can lead us to intuition. People who inspire us are always great choices for quality-time visits.

7. <u>Set some goals.</u>
The excitement of creating a goal — and knowing you have what it takes to achieve it — generates long-

---

[12] "Alone Time is Really Good for You." Mercola, Dr. Joseph. June 4, 2015. http://articles.mercola.com/sites/articles/archive/2015/06/04/alone-time.aspx.

lasting excitement, which will strengthen your desire for a better life.

8. **Try something new.**

   A fantastic way to create excitement for years to come is going out into the world and taking on a new adventure, particularly one that's really a rush. For instance, I found this review online: "I went zip-lining last month already, and was afraid of heights, but challenged myself to do it. My fear turned into excitement, and that excitement has turned into something I can tap into to this day. When I feel weighed down, I just take a quick mental escape to that adventure and can generate excitement to get me motivated to take care of business! Highly recommended." What's your "rush adventure"?

9. **Find a way to interact with people who have excitement levels you like.**

   Excitement is contagious and motivating. Yes, some people are a bit over-the-top, and think everything is like a high school cheer. But overall, we can learn some of our best skills by being around people who think positively and have a can-do attitude.

10. **Create social circles that lift you up.**

    Stagnancy stifles excitement. It's wonderful to have life-long friends, but if you're only talking about the "glory days" instead of "seizing the day," you might have a problem. You also need connections that help you in the here and now. As they say, "The past is wonderful to reflect on, but it hardly builds the future."

Excitement is a wonderful feeling that helps generate great things. By definition, it energizes you. That's why it makes sense to learn how to sustain your good energy, and drive your desires forward.

Focus on Sustaining Your Energy

When it comes to our energy and motivations, most of us start out with a bang, but end with a kerplunk. Remember, some of the reasons for this deflation include the following:

- ✓ We were in hot pursuit of the wrong things.
- ✓ We only thought we wanted what we started out pursuing.
- ✓ We realized it was not the right thing for us to work toward.
- ✓ We chickened out.
- ✓ When it came to our pursuit, we weren't fans of this sentiment: "When the going gets tough, the tough get going."

However, there is another reason that our kerplunk may have arrived before we crossed the finish line. We simply may not have had the physical energy to do what was necessary.

According to Tony Schwartz, founder and CEO of The Energy Project, "Time is a finite category, and as such, can be managed only to a certain extent. As opposed to that, our energy levels are renewable and can be influenced." [13]

How many of you make aggressive to-do lists for your day? Probably a lot. In today's world, many people have three lists:

- ✓ The written list
- ✓ The list in a word processor on your laptop
- ✓ The list on an app on your tablet or phone

Now ask yourself this: Do you get everything done on your list for that day, every day? Likely not. And why is that? This self-inflicted failure is most often due to the following:

- ✓ Not enough time
- ✓ Not planning for emergencies, or unexpected situations
- ✓ Not enough ENERGY

Another statistic that The Energy Project mentions explains the reasons behind this self-inflicted failure: 74% of employees do not have enough energy to take care of business. And let's get real: If there's not enough to take care of business, there's not enough to take care of our own needs. Often, we keep pushing our own needs to the next day, and then the next. Eventually, we send them permanently to Never Never Land. I firmly believe that

---

[13]https://theenergyproject.com/

lost ideas and thoughts should live with the Lost Boys. At least they look for new adventures, and as adults, we forget about adventure all too often.

What are some of the best ways to energize yourself and have a stellar day, not a stifle-your-yawns type of day? These ideas are wonderful for putting the wind back in your sails:

1. **Renew your energy by giving yourself a mental break during the day.**
   When we take time to step away from our responsibilities, close our eyes, take a few deep breaths, and tune out all our electronics, we can revitalize our bodies. If we repeat this process, we will actually get more done than if we had just kept plugging away. Note: For those of you who keep plugging away regardless, remember that playing the martyr card is not a good thing. What's the martyr card? When you tell everyone that you're so busy all the time that you just don't get to do things. The fact is that most people are pretty busy all the time. So to be blunt, being busy doesn't make you special. Give yourself enough energy to do what you have to with a great attitude, and devote time to building a bridge to your intuition.

2. **Get enough sleep.**
   Sleep is the best way to give our entire bodies the energy they need. When you get enough sleep, you do the following:

- ✓ Allow your brain to rest.
- ✓ Allow your body to recharge.
- ✓ Allow your muscles to relax.
- ✓ Allow yourself to wake up feeling refreshed and prepared for the day.
- ✓ Grant yourself better health.
- ✓ Reduce stress.
- ✓ Make healthier choices about food and beverages (fewer stimulants, sugars, carbs, and other foods and drinks that temporarily boost energy).

3. **<u>Exercise.</u>**

   Even though my schedule is crazy as it is, I still make sure I devote enough time to working out. For me, it means the difference between feeling energized, and feeling weighed down. When I work out, I think more clearly, move faster, and get better results. Most people are the same way. Remember, you know your schedule, and you can dictate how much time you devote to exercise. But you have options, and some exercise is better than none.

   Here are the most common time commitments for people who regularly work out:

   - ✓ Three times a week for 30 minutes each
   - ✓ Four times a week for 20 minutes each
   - ✓ Some form of daily exercise

Choose the commitment that works best for you, and start out slow. Nothing is worse for sustaining energy than being so sore that you can barely walk.

4. **Practice mindfulness.**

   Here's a basic definition of mindfulness: The mental state you achieve by focusing on your awareness at the present moment.

   Being mindful allows you to do the following:

   ✓ Give yourself the tools you need for a happy life.
   ✓ Take proactive measures to gain control of what you want in the moment.
   ✓ Practice the prevention of undesirable thoughts and actions through self-care.

   This entire practice ties into how you choose to direct and use your energy during the day. You have two choices:

   You can let negative energy absorb your actions. Negative energy is like inefficient windows in a home: It's filled with leaks, and it can be very costly to fight to keep your home warm during those cold winds!

   Or you can allow positive energy to guide how you respond to situations. Try being calm, walking away, or accepting a volatile moment for what it is. Even in the midst of chaos, you can do what you need to do.

5. **Reflect on your lifestyle.**

   In the end, it all comes down to one question: How do you treat yourself? Your energy and intuition can't force their way into your life, if you aren't energized for their entrance in a positive way. Energy and intuition can either be that person you'll avoid in the store by dodging behind a display of toilet paper, or that coworker you greet every day with a warm, genuine smile.

Are you feeling excited yet? Take a few moments to imagine yourself doing even a fraction of the things listed here. Then think about the potential you have for actually achieving what you set out to do. You don't have to dress up in a pink Energizer Bunny outfit and spin in circles banging your drum, but you can show that you have the stamina to go the distance.

And what do you use all this amazing stamina for? It shouldn't be an option to waste it on frivolous "busy work." That's why we're going to spend some time talking about ambition.

Make Your Ambitions Work for You

Ambition is something that we should all experience in our lifetimes. It can be the catalyst that gets us moving toward what we want to achieve. For example, if you don't have the ambition to adapt to the 3 Second Rule, the chances of your success are slim. However, ambition also needs to be properly addressed, because there is a stigma about it that is based on false perceptions. Too much ambition can make you seem unappealing, but too little ambition can make it seem like you just don't care. You have to learn to make it work for you in a balanced, authentic manner. Otherwise, ambition can actually set you back, not help move you forward. I'm sharing *The Parable of the Oranges* with you to demonstrate this point.[14]

The Parable of the Oranges

There was a young man who had ambitions to work for a company, because it paid very well and was very prestigious. He prepared his resume and had several interviews. Eventually, he was given an entry-level position. Then he turned his ambition to his next goal — a supervisory position, which would afford him even greater prestige and more pay. So he completed the tasks he was given. He came in early some mornings and stayed late, so the boss would see him putting in long hours.

After five years, a supervisory position became available. But to the young man's great dismay, another employee, who had only worked for the company for six months, was given the promotion. The young man was very angry, and he went to his boss and demanded an explanation.

The wise boss said, "Before I answer your questions, would you do a favor for me?"

"Yes, sure," said the employee.

"Would you go to the store and buy some oranges? My wife needs them."

[14] "Excerpt from Living with a Purpose: The Importance of 'Real Intent.'" Ridd, Randall L. Published in *Forbes Magazine*. May 22, 2016. http://www.forbes.com/sites/amyanderson/2016/05/22/what-it-takes-to-be-a-great-employee-the-parable-of-the-oranges/#79978bd72b87.

The young man agreed and went to the store. When he returned, the boss asked, "What kind of oranges did you buy?"

"I don't know," the young man answered. "You just said to buy oranges, and these are oranges. Here they are."

"How much did they cost?" the boss asked.

"Well, I'm not sure," was the reply. "You gave me $30. Here is your receipt, and here is your change."

"Thank you," said the boss. "Now, please have a seat and pay careful attention."

Then the boss called in the employee who had received the promotion and asked him to do the same job. He readily agreed and went to the store.

When he returned, the boss asked, "What kind of oranges did you buy?"

"Well," he replied, "The store had many varieties. There were navel oranges, Valencia oranges, blood oranges, tangerines, and many others. And I didn't know which kind to buy. But I remembered you said your wife needed the oranges, so I called her. She said she was having a party, and that she was going to make orange juice. So I asked the grocer which of all these oranges would make the best orange juice. He said the Valencia orange was full of very sweet juice, so that's what I bought. I dropped *them by your home on my way back to the office. Your wife was very pleased."*

"How much did they cost?" the boss asked.

"Well, that was another problem. I didn't know how many to buy, so I once again called your wife and asked her how many guests she was expecting. She said 20. I asked the grocer how many oranges would be needed to make juice for 20 people, and it was a lot. So I asked the grocer if he could give me a quantity discount, and he did! These oranges normally cost 75 cents each, but I paid only 50 cents. Here's your change and the receipt."

The boss smiled and said, "Thank you, you may go."

He looked over at the young man, who stood up, slumped his shoulders, and said, "I see what you mean." Then he dejectedly walked out of the office.

What was the difference between these two young men? They were both asked to buy oranges, and they did. You might say that the second one went the extra mile, was more efficient, or paid more attention to detail. But the most important difference had to do with real intent, rather than just going through the motions. The first young man was motivated by money, position, and prestige. The second young man was driven by an intense desire to please his employer and an inner commitment to be the best employee he could possibly be. And the outcome was obvious.

When you think about your ambition, you have to be aware of what it represents. In order to achieve what you want, you have to do what is right and of service. Just doing something because you're told to — without giving it proper and attentive effort — is a waste of time, and it's an improper use of ambition.

You could learn this lesson the hard way. One night, one of my friends and I went to a Cavs game. Afterward, he saw that he had a text from his wife. It read: "Get cold medicine for the baby." Then it specifically listed what she wanted. At the store, he picked out the first bottle of medicine he saw that said it was for the proper age. Then he dropped me off and made his way home. I saw him a few days later and asked how the baby was doing. He replied, "Better." He then explained that after he got home, he had to go back to the store and get the right medicine. That night, his motivation had been to just get something — anything would be fine. Well, it wasn't. The result was wasted time, a still-cranky baby, and likely, an irritated wife. In this situation, was saving time worth it? Definitely not! Should he have slowed down and paid attention to all the details? Definitely!

When we link our desires with our ambitions, we can create channels to do really terrific things. We will even benefit the people around us. Going the extra mile is often the best way to show the right type of ambition. Plus, it ensures that you give your best effort the first time you do something.

Here are some effective, easy-to-implement strategies that you can use to become ambitious (if you are not already), or to use your ambition in a manner that allows for maximum effectiveness.

1. **Use positive affirmations to "get you in the mood."**

   Yes, this message gets frequently repeated. But there is a reason I repeat it: Repetition is what makes the "good stuff" stick. It might sound strange that you have to "get in the mood" to be ambitious. Nevertheless, positive affirmations can help — if you use specific, short, sweet statements like these:

   - ✓ I've got this!
   - ✓ This is important to me.
   - ✓ I want to do this.
   - ✓ Good ambition will help me go the distance.

   Affirmations don't have to be spiritual and profound; they just have to get you excited about achieving what you desire.

2. **Remember everything you have to gain.**

   It's easy to think about what you have to lose, which is why those thoughts take priority in your mind. Focus on what you can gain from a combination of ambition and good, old-fashioned moxie. This concept helps you remember that the venture you're starting is definitely worth it.

3. **Kick all those excuses to the curb.**

   Excuses are lame, and no one wants to hear them. So don't make them. Stop saying things like, "I don't feel like doing this because..." Or, "My day was so hard. I just can't..." As a side note, an excuse is different than a valid reason, which states a specific, compelling reason about why something cannot be done at a given moment. For the record, valid reasons are rare, not commonplace.

4. **Give yourself parameters to keep your ambition motivated.**

   In order to achieve what you're envisioning, your ambition needs some direction. Each and every day, know what you have to do. Find a system, stick to it, and make it work for you! Take this example: You have a busy day at work, and a report is due in the morning. You don't just think, *I know...I know... I have to get to it.* You set a specific timeline to give you direction: "At 2 PM, I am going to start compiling my report." You always need to give yourself parameters for structure, and try to stick to them. Usually, you can.

5. **Find the lessons in your failure.**

   Even failure teaches you something about ambition and moving forward. It's pretty important to know what doesn't work. Then you can try the next potential solution, or find a new way to approach your desires. For instance, the first time I wrote this book, it was completely different from what you're reading now. I tweaked and adapted it, which made me a better writer in the end.

6. <u>**Appreciate success, but don't latch onto it like a leech.**</u>
It's almost a guarantee that if you experience success and dwell on it, you are going to gain the illusion that you've "made it." You'll start thinking that you'll always succeed, which isn't true. Appreciate your successes, but don't focus all your energy on them. Many more successes are waiting for you! For example, by succeeding at clarifying your intuition, you can come full-circle in your life.

Our greatest desires stem from a wonderful combination of excitement and energy. When we have the ambition to make them part of our lives, they can come true. These desires are definitely worth celebrating, and any effort to elevate yourself through energy and excitement will yield great returns, which will guide you toward your intuition.

Activating Your Desires

The word "desire" is so enticing. It reminds me of Kaa, the snake in *The Jungle Book*. It lures you in, and you become unwillingly lost in its trance. Time to snap out of it! Daydreams don't manifest desire; action does. Excitement, energy, and ambition are three building blocks that are vital to creating the bridge to your intuition. When it comes to the fourth building block in your bridge, you have everything to be eager about.

With this activity, you're going to focus on feeling the excitement. Then you'll explore your energy, and learn what it takes to live at a certain level of excitement. And lastly, we'll address the ambition that you need to make sure that your desires are fulfilled. You'll see what you can do — right now — to work toward achieving your desires.

Excitement and Focus

While excitement and focus may seem contradictory, it's time to pay attention to how you respond to excitement, what you feel, and what you show others.

- ✓ What do you physically feel happening to you when you get excited?
- ✓ What do you emotionally and mentally feel when you're excited?
- ✓ In regard to your own excitement, can you detect any patterns? Does it carry you far enough to do something helpful, or does it quickly fade away?
- ✓ Are you caught off-guard by good things that generate excitement? Why do you think you respond the way you do?
- ✓ What does your inner dialogue say about excitement? For example: Do you believe it will be short-lived, or do you think that you've arrived, and that you're on top of the world?

✓ When your friends, family, or peers are excited, how do you feel about them? Do you get a natural euphoria from being around them, or do you start your own pity party, wondering why you're not having those feelings as well?

You're in a room with friends. One of them walks in with great news: He just won $100,000. How do you think you'd respond?

_____
_____
_____

How would you like to respond differently?

_____
_____
_____

What are three things about feeling excited that you'd like to permanently sustain?
1. _____
2. _____
3. _____

What are three ways that you can sustain your excitement today? If you get stuck, think about what you can do the next time excitement comes your way. Having a plan in place is a smart way to create new approaches to life — even when challenges occur!
1. _____
2. _____
3. _____

The time for positive reinforcement has come. It will help you manifest the excitement to achieve your desires, even when your excitement and desire are completely unrelated. The energy you gain from excitement can still be transferred, and used for a great many things. It's like an instant recharge of your internal battery.

Incorporate these affirmations into your thinking and vocabulary. And allow them to inspire your actions! (Remember Appendix A.) All of these affirmations should be liberally and freely used:

- ✓ This feels great, and I'm thankful for it!
- ✓ I am going to harvest this energy to help me achieve my desires.
- ✓ Yes!
- ✓ I'm so excited. Now it's time to conquer my world. (Yes, it's *my* world.)
- ✓ Accentuate the positive.

Find affirmations for your excitement. Then do a happy dance, and say them out loud. Whether you show it to others or keep it to yourself, it's completely up to you!

Energy and Focus

It requires energy to actually do the things we want to do, whether we desire to take action or begin thinking in a new and improved way. Having enough energy means everything. It allows us to focus on the following:

- ✓ Having a stronger resolve to give everything our best effort.
- ✓ Gaining a clearer perspective on how to process all of the events in our lives.
- ✓ Pursuing our aspirations, instead of losing the steam we need to achieve them.

If you don't feel like you have enough energy to do everything you want to do, take some time to think about the people you know who do. Most of us know people who look just as collected and energized at the end of a busy day as they did at the beginning of it. It's noticeable, and often quite enviable. We wonder how they do it. Have you ever taken any steps to improve your energy levels? Have you ever been around someone who seemed to have nonstop energy, and asked them how they do it?

Think of a few ways that you can amp up your energy levels. No excuses. Feel free to take ideas from this chapter on energy, and combine them with your own thoughts here.

1. _____

2. _____

3. _____

Where do you see opportunities for lifestyle improvements? Remember that improvements may lead to fulfilling your desires, or at least determining whether or not they're genuine:

Sleep

_____

Diet

_____

Emotional Recharging

_____

Do you do enough at this point?
1. Yes
2. No

Where do you see opportunities for lifestyle improvements? Remember that improvements may lead to fulfilling your desires, or at least determining if they're genuine.

_____
_____

What's one thing you can do today to start taking action toward a healthier lifestyle?

_____
_____

Take a look at the *Energy and Focus* section again. Do you feel excited about the opportunity that some modest modifications might make to your life's results? Does this desire excite you?

Ambition and Focus

We already covered the fact that the word "ambition" isn't always viewed favorably. Here are some types of ambition:

- ✓ Having blind ambition
- ✓ Being overly ambitious
- ✓ Being under-ambitious
- ✓ Having manifested ambition

Let's start by thinking of some positive associations that include the word "ambition." I'll start out by giving you one. Then you'll come up with at least three more. Think about how you use positive ambition in your life. These words may be fantastic catalysts. They may remind you of how excitement and energy can keep you homed in on manifested ambition, and help you achieve what you desire.

What are some manifested ambitions that would benefit you?

_____

_____

_____

From the list above, which item is your favorite?

_____

And why?

_____

_____

Here's an example scenario of a visualization that includes "manifested ambition":

For the longest time, I have had a <u>desire</u> to learn more about classic art — those wonderful works from the old masters. I could have taken a few classes at the community center, and I live within a few hours of the art museum. But I just haven't done it. I keep making excuses. I could commit to <u>spending less time on social media,</u> and I could <u>let my family know that I will not be home one night a week </u>when the next class starts. So I'm going to take advantage of <u>manifested ambition</u> to pursue this desire: *I'm excited about the rewards it can offer me. This opportunity will help <u>stimulate my mind</u> and <u>keep me excited</u> about learning something new. Furthermore, it will <u>energize me</u> and keep me expanding my horizons.*

The keywords have been underlined. They invoke positive thoughts and actions, in order to turn desires into works-in-motion. You may not have the desire to learn more about classical art, but think about it: What do you desire that you've been letting pass you by? It doesn't have to be life-shattering, just life-shifting. And it should be good for you. Having fun is both good and productive. Now it's time to write down your ambition scenario — by using your favorite ambition statement, or an entirely different one. After all, good ambition is ambition worth having!

_____

_____

_____

_____

_____

_____

On a scale of 1 to 10 (10 being great), what is your excitement level about this ambition statement? _____

Is the number at least an 8 or above? If not, how can you raise your excitement to that level?

_____

_____

_____

If you are at an 8 or above, do you have three ideas about maintaining that excitement?

_____

_____

_____

On a scale of 1 to 10 (10 being great), how much new energy will it take to bring this ambition statement to fruition? _____

Do you feel like you have enough energy? If not, list three ways you can you improve your energy level:

1. _____
2. _____
3. _____

Congratulations on completing the fourth building block in your bridge to intuition. Once you complete the bridge, you will find the mother lode of intuition waiting for you on the other side. And it's always available in 3 seconds or less!

CHAPTER SIX

Drive

Having read the previous chapter, you know the importance of operating at peak "energy efficiency," in both your thoughts and physical responses. Now it's time to learn how to really use that fuel in your personal drive.

The word "drive" is somewhat subjective. It can mean something different to everyone. How about you? What style of drive do you have?

- ✓ Going for it, regardless of what "it" is.
- ✓ Moving in a forward direction — focused, and with your eyes straight ahead.
- ✓ Racing to the finish line — pedal to the metal at maximum speed.
- ✓ Cautiously making sure everything is in place, then slowly taking off. You're a master of the 30-point inspection to prepare for the journey.
- ✓ Being a "blaster." Fast and furious, you use up all your fuel the first day. Then you're too lazy to refuel, so you just keep going, even though you might run out.

I'll admit it: I naturally gravitate toward the first drive. I tend to go for it. There have been times when I've been singularly focused on attaining "it." But I've since realized that drive doesn't just involve trying to gain the most out of our lives, and going as far as we can. We also need to manage our drive, by developing self-awareness and a game plan. Drive is important. In some ways, it's everything. To skip the busy work and make a beeline to success, you have to heavily rely on intuition.

There are three main areas that make up the building blocks of drive:

- ✓ Resilience to handle life's ups and downs with confidence and grace.
- ✓ Alertness to know when the warning signals are going off.
- ✓ Motivation to use the good and the bad, which keep driving you to achieve.

If drive were an engine, each of these three components would be critical to it running optimally. And intuition would be the master mechanic, who knows how to fine-tune the engine. Then it would run as well as possible.

The Art of Resilience

When it comes to showing resilience, I am motivated by Bruce Lee, the epic martial artist and modern Eastern philosopher, who likened movement to water. Lee said: "Empty your mind, be formless, shapeless — like water. Now you put water in a cup, it becomes the cup. You put water into a bottle, it becomes the bottle. You put it in a teapot, it becomes the teapot. Now water can flow, or it can crash." Water never disappears; it shifts and adjusts to conform to its environment, while also having the power to hold its own. It is resilient, no matter what the environment brings its way.

We all have the ability to be resilient; kids have it much more so than adults. Think of a child who knows that if they keep acting a certain way, they will receive a reward. They're relentless. Whether they're throwing a tantrum or acting like an angel to get that piece of candy, they know what works. And they have the determination to see it through to the end. They are resilient in their efforts!

Now think about our lives as they are at this moment. Building the bridge to your intuition is a very worthwhile pursuit, which requires a deliberate effort to conquer any challenges you may face. Being resilient is helpful because it's an "attitude of the mind." It's a way of showing that you're in control of how you respond to your challenges, struggles, and even successes. We shouldn't dwell on success, any more than we should on failure.

Have you ever heard of Niesen Mountain in Switzerland? It's home to a stairway that consists of 11,674 continuous steps. Can you imagine the challenge of making it to the top of it? It might be even more challenging than achieving the 3 Second Rule. Imagine standing at the base of those stairs. How would you respond? Would you think about how long it would take to get to the top, and how tired you would be? Or would you think that you could do it one step at a time — by being resilient, and having the right attitude?

Life is never likely to get easier or more forgiving. Therefore, it's wise to learn to be resilient, and to adapt to life's twists and turns.

So how do you become more resilient? Does it seem tough to you? The wonderful (and likely relieving) news is that you don't have to take 11,674 steps to develop your resilience. In fact, it only takes seven.

Step 1 | Take a move toward a new place.

Feeling safe and secure is important. However, comfort becomes a problem when we stop ourselves from taking steps to grow and experience life on a grander, more fulfilling scale. Intuition helps you take these steps with confidence. And that confidence helps you become more resilient.

Step 2 | Be driven by what makes you passionate.

Here's one thing you can always rely on to make you bolder and more excited: Passion. Using passion as fuel for developing resilience is a wonderful strategy. Passion makes your inhibitions drop, and your excitement rise. It gives you a euphoric feeling to tap into. Intuition pays attention to these positive emotional highs, and helps you attain fulfillment.

Step 3 | To be purposeful, define your purpose.

When you *really* want something, you are willing to do a great deal to get it. But you aren't willing to do the same amount if you're pursuing something you only *think* you want. You say that the greatest things in life are worth waiting for. Waiting requires more than patience; it requires resilience. Your intuition will help you keep purposeful actions in your life, and help your "resilience muscle" pull you through to the end!

Step 4 | To make the journey less demanding, make a plan.

A little thought and preparation are powerful ways to keep up your resilience. The other benefit of making a plan is that it really cements what you're doing in your mind, and gives your intuition something to feed off. Perhaps you stare down at something and think: *I wish I'd done "this" before I did "that."* Imagine how much better it would be to instantly think: *Maybe I better check "this" before I do "that."*

Step 5 | Don't intentionally surround yourself with "downers."

You can pick and choose some of the people in your life, but others are just there, whether they're good for you or not. Watch out for people trying to squash your dreams and rain on your parade: **No one has to impact you if you don't let them**. Resilience helps. And the acknowledgment that your intuition is looking out for you helps, too!

Step 6 | Manage your mindset until you master it.

If you don't take efforts to manage your mindset, you might stumble upon success, but you won't obtain it with certainty. You might get by with negative attitudes and pessimistic thoughts, but they'll never lift you up. Basically, there's no excuse: You *can* give yourself the proper mindset, develop resilience, and further close the gap between your ego-driven willpower and intuition.

Step 7 | Let's get "physical"!

A well-rested body equals a well-rested mind. With enough rest, you'll be able to take on the demanding tasks that are involved in making it through the day. Furthermore, some of your best creative ideas and motivating moments can happen when you're exercising (including sex). Every step toward resilience is easier when you're not afraid to get physical!

***

When you're the teacher showing yourself how to achieve positive outcomes, you're going to view your mental ingenuity, your resilience, and this book as valuable resources. Just imagine controlling and cultivating these things:

- ✓ Gaining the right attitude to help you get caught up when you fall behind.
- ✓ Having the self-discipline to get yourself back on track.
- ✓ Acknowledging when you've taken strides forward in your pursuits.
- ✓ Being better prepared to keep learning and growing.
- ✓ Offering positive, internal, emotional support.
- ✓ Dealing with life better.
- ✓ Using the one-two punch of resilience and intuition to be more efficient, happier, and more productive.

Suddenly, Niesen Mountain's 11,674 steps don't seem so daunting, do they? You know exactly how to strategize a plan and stick with it!

Resilience is amazing for delivering the following:

- ✓ Increased confidence
- ✓ Stronger problem-solving abilities
- ✓ Reasons to celebrate
- ✓ Ways to take advantage of natural excitement and enthusiasm
- ✓ Techniques for stopping overwhelmed, stifled feelings

This concept is so exciting, because it really makes or breaks any journey you choose to take, especially the ones along the bridge to your intuition.

Being Alert in a Hectic World

There are days when everything just gets to be too much, and all you long for is your "Calgon moment." Take me away! Sure, it's good to be able to separate yourself from the chaos of the world when you need a break. Sometimes, a break is mandatory – because if you don't take it, you might break down. However, there are other times when you need to put on the brakes, and just take it all in.

Then you can learn that:

- ✓ Your experiences are what you make them.

- ✓ Oftentimes, the hectic world you see is of your own making.
- ✓ Chaos can be exciting.
- ✓ Likewise, chaos can be overwhelming.

In the end, you really need to look at everything around you, and see what is really happening. At times, your emotions dictate what you believe you're seeing, and other times, the "visual facts" don't always paint the correct picture. But you'll never know for sure, if you don't pay attention to it all.

To be alert, you need to learn how to properly evaluate the events and situations in your life. Your perceptions are based on a combination of the following:

- ✓ Your positive experiences
- ✓ Your bad choices
- ✓ Choices that others make, which affect us

Now think of drive as an engine again. The way you process things in a hectic world is the gunk that builds up in your gears. By taking time to evaluate your perceptions, ensure you are looking at things in a balanced way, and refrain from indulging in emotional thinking, you can clear out that gunk, and make sure that your engine keeps running smoothly.

According to the University of Massachusetts Dartmouth, there are seven steps in the decision-making process:[15]

Step 1 | Identify the decision.
Try to clearly define the decision you must make. This first step is very important.

Step 2 | Gather relevant information.
List the information you need, the sources you're going to use, and the methods you're going to implement to get them. This step involves both internal and external work. Some information is internal: You'll seek it through a process of self-assessment. Other information is external: You'll find it online, in books, through conversations, or in other sources.

Step 3 | Identify the alternatives.
As you collect information, you'll probably identify several alternative paths of action. You can also use your imagination, as well as any information you've gathered, to construct even more alternatives. During this step, you'll list all possible and desirable alternatives.

Step 4 | Weigh the evidence.
To imagine completing each of the alternatives, draw on your information and emotions. Would all the alternatives resolve the need identified in Step 1? As you go through this difficult, internal process, you'll begin favoring certain alternatives, including the ones that seem

---

[15]Decision-making process. University of MA-Dartmouth. 2016.
http://www.umassd.edu/fycm/decisionmaking/process/.

to have a higher possibility of reaching your goal. Finally, place the alternatives in order of priorities, based on your own value system.

Step 5 | Choose from the alternatives.
Once you've weighed all the evidence, you're ready to select the alternative that should be best for you. You might even choose a combination of alternatives. It's likely that your choice in Step 5 will be the first item in the list from Step 4.

Step 6 | Take action.
You're now ready to take positive action. Begin implementing the alternative you chose in Step 5.

Step 7 | Review your decision and its consequences.
In this final step, consider the results of your decision, and evaluate whether or not it's resolved the need you identified in Step 1. If the decision has **not** met the identified need, you may want to repeat certain steps of the process to make a new decision. For example, you might want to gather more detailed (or somewhat different) information, or explore additional alternatives.

I think most of us can agree that the research faculty at the University of Massachusetts Dartmouth are pretty smart, and understand how to solve problems and analyze situations.

When you look at those seven steps, do you:

✓ Think they seem difficult?

- ✓ Think they seem complicated?
- ✓ Doubt your ability to successfully navigate them?
- ✓ See how they could help *if* you were successful at following them?

By committing to these steps (which are highly complementary to all the steps you've been learning in this book), you'll find that they eventually become second-nature. And when that happens, Dr. Seuss' parade down Mulberry Street will be happening in your mind, and you'll be the Grand Marshal of it all. You'll be the Master of the 3 Second Rule!

Powered by Motivation

If anyone knows about maintaining powerful drive to cross the finish line, it's Mario Andretti. He's set some amazing records. It seems like he was born to drive a race car. In case you're somehow not familiar with him, he's:

- One of the most famous American racers.
- One of only two drivers to have won races in Formula One, IndyCar, World Sportscar Championship, and NASCAR.

If there's a type of auto race, chances are that he's not only participated in it, but mastered it enough to win. Does this accomplishment take natural talent? Sure! Guess what else it takes? A whole lot of motivation.

Being motivated is dependent on how we're feeling at a given time. According to research:

"When experimental subjects are told of an unhappy event, but then instructed to try not to feel sad about it, they end up feeling worse than people who are informed of the event, but given no instructions about how to feel."[16]

We generate our motivations from our emotions. The more eager we are for something, the more motivated we are. This finding tells us two important things about being motivated: *We need to know how we feel about it, and where those feelings stem from.*

To determine what's going on with our emotions, consider these three points of awareness:

1. **Find a way to be positive about everything.**
    While it's easy to be positive when you're motivated, the same can't be said for anything you're resistant to doing. However, by acknowledging our feelings, you can approach these tasks positively. *You can become who you want to be.* And even if it's something as simple as washing your window sills in the spring, you can do it.

2. **Consider a good, reasonable way to reward yourself.**
    Hey, you're human, so you love rewards. Hands down, they do more to motivate you than just about

[16] *The Antidote: Happiness for People Who Can't Stand Positive Thinking.* Burkeman, Oliver. Farrar, Straus and Giroux; First Edition. November 13, 2012.

anything else. When we were kids, you probably got a sticker when you performed well. As an adult, you can also give yourself something that you really love when you do well. And it doesn't have to cost a lot of money. What do you really enjoy that fits within your budget – or is completely free of charge? One of my friends has found an appealing option: She rewards herself by taking time to devote her full attention to something she loves. Therefore, she has higher-quality relationships, finds constant sources of inspiration, and continues to be motivated to do great things.

Think outside the box!

3. **Recruit people to hold you accountable.**
   Although everything you do has to start with yourself, there is no shame in finding people to hold you accountable. For example: If you want to lose a bit of your "excess tummy," you might take ten minutes every night to do some crunches. Tell your spouse, friends, or kids to remind you if they haven't seen you doing them. And promise them this: When they remind you, you'll be grateful for it, not nasty about it. That's only reasonable, right?

How are you feeling about motivation? Remember, these are fundamental parts of finding the right type of motivation for you: Knowing who you are and working with yourself as you are!

By being resilient and alert, you can find the motivation that drives you to the prize you're waiting for: A subconscious mind that has an awesome relationship with your intuition. Let the 3 Second Rule adopt you, just like you're trying to adopt it!

Activating Your Drive

Sometimes, you have to put the gas pedal down, and really start exploring how to get where you want to go. Imagine that you're a Grand Prix driver, ready to start the race. The course is filled with twists, turns, obstacles, and loads of other traffic. Everyone wants the same thing. What will you do to stand out? What will deter you, and what won't? You need to plan ahead, and build up your intuition. You need to make split-second decisions to prevent you from crashing, help you gain the advantage, and eventually cross that finish line.

With this activity, you are going to learn how to get your drive going by better understanding yourself and your actions. When things go badly, do you have the resilience to climb out of the hole you're in? When you encounter someone with road rage, do you have the alertness to anticipate it, and diffuse the situation? And when your gas tank is nearing empty, are you motivated to fill it up right away? By the time you finish the following exercises, you're going to know how to get your drive going by better understanding yourself and your actions.

A Driving Resilience

Some of us think we're so tough that we can handle anything that comes our way. Others feel that they're not equipped to handle anything. Are either of these extremes true? Everyone handles some things well, and struggles with other things. Questioning your resilience helps you learn how you're tough, and how you could be tougher. What are your resilience levels in the following situations?

Scenario 1: The Really Bad News

You just did something that you've been told not to do for a long time now, and you got caught: You were texting and rear-ended a car with a mom and her two little kids in it. She's worried about her kids, and you're grateful that everyone is okay. When the officers arrive, it's time to confess. If you don't say what you were doing, they'll find out. They have cameras everywhere now. As expected, you get a few hefty reminders of what you've done: One ticket for speeding, and another for inattentive driving. Your insurance premiums go up. Finally, your name is in the paper. Your friends know what happened, so you're embarrassed. And the real kicker is that the person you hit is the sister-in-law of one of your coworkers.

Time to think...

> ✓ In the aftermath of this situation, how would you handle your emotions?

✓ Would you hang your head low, and stay out of sight as much as you could, until people forgot?

✓ Would you be sorry about what you did, or only sorry that you got caught?

✓ Would you make excuses, or just buck up and accept your mistake?

✓ How would you find the comfort to get through the turbulence of the situation?

Here's how resilient people would respond to this situation: They would feel horrible about what happened, and have a bit of self-pity. But they would also realize that they cannot dwell in the past, and can only learn from what happened. After a genuine and heartfelt apology, they would commit to not making that mistake again, and they would use what happened as a learning tool. If their emotions were off-kilter from what happened, they'd take action to sort out those feelings. They might pray, meditate, talk with a friend, or exercise. They wouldn't allow it to stifle them. Furthermore, if they're attuned enough (which resilient people are), they would realize that somewhere in their subconscious mind, they already warned themselves not to do it.

Were you resilient in your answers?

Scenario 2: The Heart that Plummeted

You're in a long-term relationship (either married or committed), and you feel really happy. Overall, communication is clear, fighting is healthy and minimal, and things flow pretty well (especially when you compare your relationship to some of your friends' relationships). Then one day, your love comes home and says, "We need to talk." It turns out that the two of you are not on the same page at all, and your partner is set to move on and start a new chapter without you. It shocks you. You're devastated and heartbroken. You ache all over and feel emotionally numb.

Time to think...

- ✓ Do you discredit your partner's feelings, and chalk them up to a personal crisis of some sort?
- ✓ Are you instantly in negative mode, wondering: "What's wrong with me?" Or were you always waiting for the other shoe to drop, because you knew deep down that it was too good to be true?
- ✓ Do you start screaming and yelling until you burst out into tears?
- ✓ Are you angry enough that you just walk away, and end the painful conversation?
- ✓ Do you start casting blame and throwing out accusations about how lucky your partner was to have you?

A resilient response to this kind of tough, unexpected news would be to release your emotions (which is completely okay to do). Then take a deep breath. If you need to process everything, walk away. After all, your partner has obviously thought this through. Recognize that you can't change his or her feelings, and trying to do so will not make you feel better. You can't make partners change their minds and love you like before. It may take a few days or weeks, but you will eventually realize that you can take control of your misery. If you're mad as hell, admit it. But use your anger to your advantage. (Take note: That doesn't mean that you should be vengeful.)

Would you handle this situation with a resilient mindset?

***

What have you had to deal with that was very tough on you, and impacted your mood, attitude, and actions? It could be recent, or something from a while ago.

_____

_____

_____

Describe how you handled the situation, taking into account the strong emotions, the struggles, and the actions you took because of your emotions.

_____

_____

_____

What are three ways that you either used (or could have used) resilience to make the situation better?

1. _____
2. _____
3. _____

If you enjoy using reminders to stay on the sunny side, these resilience-rooted affirmations may be just what you need:

- ✓ I am in complete control of myself.
- ✓ My mind is strong, capable, and disciplined.
- ✓ Resilience comes naturally to me.
- ✓ Having control over my impulses is easy for me.
- ✓ Life's storms cannot best me.

It's worth doing whatever it takes, for you to develop resilience.

Alert at the Wheel

Pay attention! Wow, there is so much going on all the time, both within you and all around you. Most people miss out on magic moments in their lives, simply because they weren't alert enough. Don't be that person. Being alert makes you a better all-around individual. Then you'll be a stronger partner, a more fulfilled parent, and a more proactive advocate. Being alert is important to maintaining your quality of life, as well as your connectedness to an intuitive state of existence.

Do you feel alert about what's happening in your life emotionally? Explain.

_____
_____
_____

Do you feel alert about the world around you? Explain.

_____
_____
_____

What are three things you could do to become a more alert person? Factor in everything that you've learned in this book. There are hints everywhere!

1. _____
2. _____
3. _____

On a scale of 1 to 10 (1 being low, and 10 being high), how would you rate your alertness? _____.

Is this number acceptable? Why or why not?

_____

_____

Motivated to Keep the Drive Alive

The outcome of any situation is linked to your motivation. The things we love best are the things we often shine at, because we're constantly motivated to give them our best effort. How many times have you thought: *If they gave as much effort to <u>fill in the blank</u> as they give to <u>fill in the blank</u>, they'd be a lot better off.* Of course, that person may have a different definition of "better off" than we do. The point is that we noted the results of that person's level of motivation.

Put a little thought into these questions:

- ✓ What motivates me most, and why?
- ✓ When I am motivated and unmotivated, what are the differences in my results?

✓ Are there ways I can harvest my motivators to improve other areas of my life (or to pursue my goals)?

✓ What value do I place on motivation?

Is your motivation helpful to you, or does it hold you back? Why?

_____

_____

_____

List three ways that you can be more motivated to do the things you struggle with:

1. _____

2. _____

3. _____

Take a few moments, and visualize what it will be like to home in on your motivations. Then you can achieve something you've never been successful at before. Maybe it's a permanent state of fitness, a promotion, a new hobby, or a volunteer position. Make it personal to you, so you'll demonstrate why it's important!

_____

_____

_____

Finally, what's one thing that you can do today that's motivating? Think of this thing as the fuel for your drive. Ready, set, go!

_____

_____

_____

Congratulations on completing the fifth building block in your bridge to intuition. You're beginning to fine-tune your engine, and learning to go where you want to. Next, you're going to learn about the art of discipline, including how self-discipline can actually be quite enjoyable! Yes, you read that correctly.

CHAPTER SEVEN

Discipline

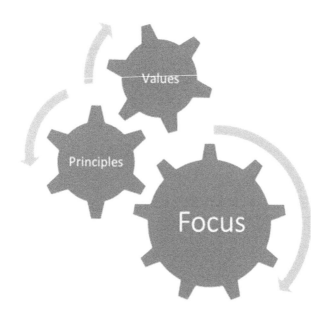

Here's the deal... Your day is going to start whether or not you participate. Short of death, there's no way to stop tomorrow from arriving. And no, pulling the covers over your head and hoping the day forgets about you will not stop a new day from beginning. So why would anyone choose not to make the most of it? Why dwell on what's funky and dysfunctional, instead of thinking about how to make it better?

Are you asking, "But is that *really* possible?" Yes, it can be done! You have to use self-discipline to do it, but by using it, you'll find that you really can do what you've set your conscious and subconscious minds on.

For the most part, the word "discipline" doesn't have positive associations. We view discipline as hard work, and it certainly can be. But it's also rewarding, as it helps generate great results, such as achieving a goal or finishing a project.

Discipline is beneficial, too. Consider this:

1. **It helps you focus.**
   By knowing that you need to do something, and holding yourself accountable for doing it, you become more focused. Then the chances of successfully completing the project are higher.

2. **You'll earn respect.**
   You will be noticed and respected if you are disciplined and do what's required of you.

3. **It can help you achieve a healthier lifestyle.**
   Wouldn't you love to stop after only one cookie, or easily recognize that a bit of exercise feels better than lying on the couch like a lump? These actions require discipline and lead to a healthier, more vibrant lifestyle.

4. **It helps you have better self-control.**
   In other words, stop yourself from doing things that may have a detrimental impact on you. For example, if you're financially strapped, don't allow yourself to alleviate stress by buying a new blouse that you don't need.

5. **You'll make more out of opportunities to learn.**
   Consistent learning and growth require discipline. This truism remains consistent, whether you want to go back to school to earn a degree, or learn the 3 Second Rule.

6. **You'll make better use of your time.**
   By being disciplined about your schedule, you can stop procrastinating and make better use of your time. You will then have more free time to do things you actually enjoy, such as spending time with friends or family, taking on a new hobby, and taking better care of yourself.

7. **You'll have less stress and anxiety.**
   Self-discipline helps control (and often eliminates) stress and anxiety in your life. This statement can be true in both your personal and professional lives. For example, if you're at risk for heart disease, it takes discipline to cut down on unhealthy fats. Cutting down on fats isn't easy, despite the obvious risks. But when you do, your stress can significantly decrease.

Are you starting to see how self-discipline can really impact your outcome? It's connected to everything, just as intuition is.

The best way to create self-discipline is to focus on the person you are, and what's of value to you. This focus involves:

- ✓ Knowing your values
- ✓ Understanding the principles that drive your inner patience
- ✓ Focusing on the intuitive process

Through these three areas, you zoom in on the most effective ways to become more disciplined. The results really do lead to feelings of self-worth and achievement. These feelings also help you reconnect with your intuition, so you can begin using it.

Your "Values Summit"

You'd be hard-pressed to find an adult who doesn't know what values are. Furthermore, most people would acknowledge that they are necessary to living a sounder life. But many of us don't act in a way that proves that we really mean what we say about our values. You know how it goes: Cutting a corner here and there, and making an "exception" to your own rule.

I've found it beneficial to think of values as being unwavering. Then if you depart from them, you know you're making a wrong turn, or taking the easy way out.

A quote I recently came across stated this concept perfectly: "Our values are important because they help us to grow and develop. They help us create the future we want to experience."[17]

For us, in the here and now, we need to develop an intuition that will complement our values, and help us make better choices that truly reflect our values.

Here are three important things that our values offer us:

- ✓ Values are a guide to our personal ethics.
  What can we do in good conscience, and what will we refuse to do?
- ✓ Values demonstrate integrity.
  Our integrity establishes our credibility. Do people know that you'll deliver what you say you will? Do they count on you to stand by what you believe?
- ✓ Values are blueprints that help us create visions that become a reality.
  When you structure your pursuits around your values, you're giving yourself a better chance to authentically succeed. Do you prefer a journey on the right path, or one in the fast lane that will lead to a dead end for your pursuits?

When it comes to values, there is no better place to look than the recent stories about real estate fraud. These

---

[17]Barrett Values Centre. 2016. https://www.valuescentre.com/mapping-values/values/why-values-are-important.

stories are everywhere, but if you haven't heard them, let me share one with you. It pinpoints the "value" of adhering to your values.

Before the real estate bubble burst, it was easy to buy and sell property. This situation was great, but it led a lot of people — both experts in the industry and ordinary consumers — to view real estate as an instant financial return, rather than a slowly building, long-term investment. This practice is called flipping houses.

Many times, agents would sell a house for an inflated price, and give the difference to investors/buyers/negotiators, in exchange for the deal. The result was a lot of overpriced houses on the market, and people with loans they couldn't possibly fulfill. For a lot of people, this whole practice led to disastrous credit decisions, as well as some criminal charges. If you asked any of those people if it was really worth it, what do you think they would say?

The odds are excellent that they would acknowledge (in that glorious 20/20 hindsight) that it was not worth it at all. It cost them credibility, trust, relationships, financial status, and perhaps even freedom.

Now ask yourself: *How could this entire situation have been avoided?* The answer: *By sticking to your values, and not taking the easy route to financial gain.* If it was easy to get rich, everyone would do it, right? Even the laziest person can probably do a small task, if it means they have enough money to sit around and keep being lazy.

Thankfully, that's not you. And if you're learning anything from this book, you know it isn't me, either.

Values are everything.

Let me repeat that again: Values are everything!

Know this truth, accept it, and begin living by it to the best of your ability. When your intuition really begins working for you, you will want to know that it's working toward the right things!

According to Richard Barrett of The Barrett Values Centre, "Over time, humans have developed six ways of making decisions — instincts, subconscious beliefs, conscious beliefs, values, intuition, and inspiration."

Based on Barrett's research, there are four stages involved in decision-making: 1) data-gathering; 2) information-processing; 3) meaning-making; and 4) decision-making.[18]

Let's break these stages down:

- ✓ Your five senses are used to gathering data from your external environment.
- ✓ You move on to processing information, which involves the brain assembling and processing the

---

[18]"The Six Modes of Decision Making." Barrett, Richard. https://www.valuescentre.com/sites/default/files/uploads/Six_Modes_of_Decision-Making.pdf

data received from your senses. In turn, the mind creates a database for all the information you've gathered.

✓ It's time to gather meaning from the data. During this stage, your brain is being used by your mind, ego, and soul. At this point, your values are really key, as they'll help you determine a meaning.

Your decision is made. Everything is gathered and processed, so you make your decision, based on the computations of your mind and soul.

Regarding the modes of decision-making that Barrett highlights, I want to share one in particular with you: "Instinct-based decision-making takes place at the atomic/cellular level, because the actions that arise are based on learned DNA responses, principally associated with issues of survival."

Let's get our instincts back! It all begins with defining your values. Here are a few steps to help you do just that:

1. **<u>Begin contemplating what your core values may be.</u>**

   To accomplish this goal, you will need to allot some time to it. Some goals may be easy to determine, but others may take a while. An example would be a serious debate about your perspectives on some of the hot-button issues.

First, ask yourself: What's the most important thing in my life?

Next, ask yourself: What do the most important things in my life mean to me?

For example, if you chose money as a core value in your life, begin by asking yourself: What does money mean to you? And why? Your answer might be: It means economic freedom, security, and success.

The core value in this example is not the money itself. It's what the money brings: Economic freedom, security, and success.

2. **Choose which of your values you really want to focus on.**

    Typically, there should be no more than seven values. If you choose too many, you may end up restricting yourself. You will also make it harder for your intuition to work toward these values in the way you want them to!

    Prioritize your values in order of importance. (The highest priority should be #1.) If you struggle with these priorities, ask yourself the following question: If I had to live my life without one of these things, which one would I be most willing to give up? (This thing should be the lowest-priority item on your list.)

3. **Commit to embracing and using your defined core values.**

   Do whatever you can to remember them on a conscious level, until your subconscious mind knows they're part of your very fiber. From that point on, you'll succeed. And in the last part of this chapter, you'll complete some exercises to put it all together!

Knowing your values should be a common skill, but sadly, it's not. That's why this step is fundamentally important when learning to use your intuition. To help you put it all together, we're going to delve into how you can participate in an "inner practice" to help ensure success.

Principles of Your Inner Practice

Few things are more annoying than being around someone who just talks, talks, talks about what they are doing to get better. Meanwhile, you clearly see that they're failing on the do, do, do!

Through discipline, we move from talk to action. Discipline is a recurring theme — both in this book and in life. Look at how many quotes out there cite some version of this idea. The message is a good one, and it's meant to sink in, sometimes despite ourselves.

The discipline and courage that it takes to understand our driving values are so important, and it can never be undermined as being "insignificant" or "meaningless."

<u>Lily's Story</u>

Lily grew up in a household where she was neither lifted up, nor encouraged to explore her fullest potential. While some parents would encourage their children's best efforts, her parents would say, "You're hopeless." They were products of their upbringings, of course. Negativity can spread like wildfire, run amok, and become part of a person's thoughts about themselves. Keep in mind that her parents were adults who should have taken responsibility for their own actions, but they just didn't take this fact into consideration. Perhaps they didn't want others to succeed, because they felt unsuccessful.

Despite the way Lily was treated, she still had a strong work ethic as a young adult. She was never late to her job, and always offered as many extra hours to her job as she could, even though it was just fast-food. She was a great team member. Admittedly, she worked that hard because it was better to be at work than at home, but that's okay!

One day, Lily's manager came up to her and asked, "Lily, there's a position for a weekend assistant manager opening up. I'd like you to apply for it if you're interested."

"What? Me?" she asked in genuine disbelief.

"Yes, you." The manager told her that she was a great worker, was liked by everyone, and really showed a commitment to being responsible. They appreciated everything she did.

Lily should have been able to graciously accept the compliment, and should not have acted shocked that her best efforts had been noticed. But it felt so unnatural to her. Her low self-worth and fear of failure stopped her from applying for that job. But her manager, bless his heart, brought it up again. And then again. Eventually, she did apply.

Do you know what Lily found out?

The application was a mere formality. She was offered the job the second she handed over the application. She was shocked, but it jolted her with a good feeling. She became aware of how she felt, and she realized that this low self-worth was a real disservice to her. Of course, she still had a habit of negative self-talk. But now she was aware of the habit. Isn't that what most of us hope for: To know what we need to know?

Lily went into the management position with a great deal of fear, and she didn't know if she had the ability to be respected. But she kept working with the integrity that earned her the job in the first place.

Ultimately, Lily was promoted even further up the ranks of the organization. And with each step she took, her sense of inner hopelessness grew into a sense of inner strength.

What does Lily's story remind us of? There are two things that really stand out to me:

1. We are often so hard on ourselves about our own efforts. Remember, we don't have to give anyone else the power to damage our internal healthiness. As soon as we recognize what's going on, we can begin building the strength to kick those people's negativity to the curb. We may still have to deal with them in our lives, but they do not have to dictate our self-worth.

2. Often, the messages and signs we need to hear don't come from the people close to us. Instead, they come from people who we may not even realize are paying attention.

And always remember: People are typically too selfish to give false compliments. When you receive a compliment, take it with a sincere heart of gratitude. It helps strengthen inner patience as you grow stronger.

If it's just too hard for you to think that anyone could give you a real compliment, remember this: That's your problem, not theirs. Use good words to develop good internal motivation. It takes discipline, but it does result in sweet rewards, including a stronger, healthier, and more intuitive self.

Focus on the Intuitive Process

Steve Jobs called intuition "more powerful than intellect." If that sentiment is good enough for him, it's probably good enough for us, too — especially when you consider that he's thought of as one of the smartest tech guys of all time. With his innovative mind, and the right people around him, he changed our world. And he didn't just turn the impossible into the possible; he turned it into the everyday! Back in November 2014, Apple announced that it had sold its billionth iOS device.[19] Wow! Since the world population is now approximately 7.5 billion, Apple is now a part of approximately 1 out of 7 people's lives.

There are a few examples that show the power of the intuitive process even more than that. Jobs had a vision, saw a demand, and certainly demonstrated the discipline to stick with it. With his passing, his work has been taken over by others, but it will never be forgotten or ignored. The fact that he prioritized intuition to that degree cannot be ignored!

What about you? Do you have a big idea waiting to be developed by using your intuition? I bet you do. It may not be worth millions of dollars, but is there a price tag on the betterment of your life? Not to me!

---

[19] 1 billion Apple devices are in active use around the world. Statt, Nick. January 26, 2016. http://www.theverge.com/2016/1/26/10835748/apple-devices-active-1-billion-iphone-ipad-ios.

Do you know what your intuitive process is? You may not be outwardly aware of it, and that's okay. But you want to make sure it's there. Therefore, consider these inspiring ideas, and acknowledge that your discipline is doing its due diligence for your intuition.

Listen to Your Intuition.
In its broadest sense, this concept is the topic of this book. The next time you hear your intuition belting out an idea, do it a favor and listen.

Take Time for Solitude.
Alone time is zone time. When you zone in, you can home in on what's happening in your life. Maybe you see the "writing on the wall," or recognize that you're willing something to happen that's actually detrimental to you.

Be Creative.
In my life, creativity is a must. When you're creative, you're using gifts that you're naturally given and/or have developed (and sometimes suppress), in order to do something good for your energy, spirit, self-confidence, and self-fulfillment. Intuition loves creativity, as it offers different avenues to do great things.

Be Mindful.
Always be an advocate for understanding your environment and your responses to it. Mindfulness is necessary for good decision-making, including the discipline to handle life's events in a meaningful, proactive manner.

Observe Your World.

Inspiration is often a glance away. There are many powerful stories about people who changed their outlook on life — and therefore their destiny — by doing simple things. It's inspiring to see how simple things often lead to grand results. Likewise, you can finally take your parents' advice: "Learn from my mistakes. Don't repeat them."

Know Your Body.

Our bodies reflect stress and anxiety, and they will tell us if we are not living to our full potentials. Always be mindful of the following:

- ✓ Your weight
- ✓ How much or little you eat
- ✓ The amount of alcohol you consume
- ✓ Your sleeping patterns
- ✓ Your energy levels

If you don't heed these things, your relationships will be impacted, and your career and personal life will likely bring unnecessary challenges your way. While some challenges can be wonderful and invigorating, these challenges can lead to losing a job, losing a relationship, or separating yourself from those who want to be there for you!

Heed Your Dreams.

No good dream should be wasted. If you're blessed with a vision of something you want to do, can do, or are compelled to do, don't let it go to waste. Have the discipline to take action!

Create Meaningful Connections.
By gaining the discipline to know yourself, your values, and your intuitive self, you can truly create meaningful connections with others. I hope this book is allowing me to connect with you, and that what I've shared will ultimately be of great value to you.

Acknowledge and Release Negative Emotions.
It's important not to focus on the negative, but it's just as important to acknowledge negativity. If something doesn't sit right with you, don't pretend that it does. Give it weight, and take a positive approach to changing it.

Here's a great example: Someone doesn't like the way their (local, state, or federal) government is operating. So they run for office to try to change it. If their platform is built on their values and convictions, they'll probably have the discipline to give it their best effort. If so, others could see the benefits of their message.

Make Sure You Have Downtime.
Downtime is different than alone time. With downtime, you quite literally "let it all go." You stop treating everything so damn seriously, and enjoy yourself. You take a break from worrying about that D on your kid's report card. You forget about the snarky comment your coworker made, and your even snarkier response.

In that moment, the fact that your ex dumped you for someone fifteen years younger doesn't matter. Your mind is not a stormy sea, but a calm and tranquil bay. Aah!

Activating Your Discipline

According to an online dictionary, discipline is defined as "the practice of training people to obey rules or a code of behavior, using punishment to correct disobedience." While training people is a good thing when it's helpful, training yourself is "the bomb"! You have to take care of your own needs first. Only then can you take care of others.

As far as punishment goes, know this: no one can ever punish us worse than we punish ourselves. We are often the corporal disciplinarians in our minds. It doesn't have to be this way. These exercises are guarantees that you'll transition away from that corporal mindset, as long as you have the discipline to invest in you!

Through values, principles, and determination, you can begin recognizing and creating opportunities that you'll have the drive to see through to the end. And the end is really just the beginning of a better life, a stronger sense of purpose, and an everlasting connection with your intuition!

Vividly Defined Values

What do your values really mean to you? The following questions should help you reflect on this concept. They'll help define the best course of action, which will help you build your bridge to intuition.

- ✓ If someone asked you what your core values are, would you be able to quickly and decisively answer them?
- ✓ When you think of values, do you see them as roadblocks, or as guides to a positive life? And why?
- ✓ Do you struggle with not knowing what's truly important to you? In challenging situations, do you fear that you won't stand up for what you value?
- ✓ What great experiences have you had that involved standing up for something you valued?
- ✓ Have you ever felt like you lost out on something because you chose to go with your values, instead of your temptations?
- ✓ When you hear something that contradicts your current values, do you consciously recognize it as such?

What are your thoughts about people who are clearly driven by their values?

_____

_____

_____

How would you like to see your core values add worth to your life?

_____

_____

_____

When determining the seven values that you most want to focus on in life, remember to ask yourself these two questions:

- ✓ What's most important to me?
- ✓ What do the most important things in my life mean to me?

Here's an example: Having money will give me financial freedom, security, and a sense of success. Remember, money isn't the value. Rather, financial freedom, security, and a sense of success are.

What are your core values? It may take you a few days to complete this list, but don't skip this step!

1. _____

2. _____

3. _____

4. _____

5. _____

6. _____

7. _____

What are the Top 3 Values on your list? List them out, from most to least important:

1. _____
2. _____
3. _____

Now complete a few steps, in order to further define your Top 3 Values:

Define Value #1. (Example: I value financial freedom, because it will allow me to have adventures in my life, and pay for my children's college education.)

_____
_____
_____

Write a statement about what this core value personally means to you:

_____
_____
_____

At the end of your life, you look back on this core value. What do you see?

_____
_____
_____

Define Value #2:

_____
_____
_____

Write a statement about what this core value personally means to you.

_____

_____

_____

At the end of your life, you look back on this core value. What do you see?

_____

_____

_____

Define Value #3:

_____

_____

_____

Write a statement about what this core value personally means to you.

_____

_____

_____

At the end of your life, you look back on this core value. What do you see?

_____

_____

_____

How can you keep your Core Values at the forefront of you mind? Since you have to hold yourself accountable, come up with at least three techniques that you believe you'll truly have the discipline to carry out:

1. _____

_____

2. _____

_____

3. _____

_____

Statements that reinforce your core values during trying times can be great tools for keeping your values working for you, which will help you communicate with your intuition. They're powerful reminders that you have the patience and discipline to do the right thing. Here are some examples:

- ✓ I value _____ because it provides me with _____.
- ✓ My value system is my code of honor.
- ✓ I choose values, in order to maintain self-respect.
- ✓ If something doesn't align with my values, it doesn't align with my intuitive common sense.
- ✓ I trust myself to live by my values.

Regarding your commitment to values, go big, and be bold. They're like the steel bolts that will hold your bridge to intuition together.

Perpetuating Principles

You can't instantly become a person of principle. Rather, if you're becoming this kind of person, it means that you're exercising the discipline to carry yourself forward (in a direction defined by you). And you're demonstrating that you're in control of your internal dialogue, including how it impacts your actions. Who's the boss? You're the boss!

If you live a principle-based life, you'll show wonderful attributes, including the following:

- ✓ **A sense of control over your actions and responses.** You don't explode over mistakes and misfortunes. Instead, you step away, assess, and remember that you're only human.
- ✓ **Leadership skills.** You strive to find principled solutions to any challenge, and are able to build a value-driven environment in your life.
- ✓ **The ability to give guidance that can be trusted.** You will be sought out for solutions and feedback.
- ✓ **The ability to be a great mentor.** If you operate on principle, you understand how helpful this quality is. You find joy in being of service, and spreading the word about the role of intuition during decision-making and overall fulfillment.

- ✓ **The ability to find grace in your life and in the lives of others.** It's true: To err is human; to forgive, divine.
- ✓ **The ability to accept your own responsibility for both good and bad outcomes.** Everyone experiences both failure and success, and you need to take appropriate responsibility for both. This balance will give you the mentality to level the playing field in your life.

What principles do you live by?

_____

_____

_____

_____

Do the people who know you best know your principles? Explain.

_____

_____

_____

_____

Do you like perception of your principles?
1. Yes
2. No

Why or why not?

_____

_____

Do you want to modify the ways that your principles apply to your life?

1. Yes
2. No

Why or why not?

_____

_____

What one step can you can take to redefine the principles you live by?

_____

_____

When you reflect on how you answered these questions, are you surprised by your principles? How much of an impact do they really have on your life? It's very interesting and enlightening to be aware of this impact. The way you feel about your principles at this moment is also how your subconscious mind feels about them. Your intuition feeds off it as it guides you.

Focus Pocus

Picture this: You're staring in a mirror, looking yourself right in your eyes, and loudly declaring, "Focus!" Your hands are emphasizing your point, and your mind is begrudgingly agreeing to give you what you want: Focus. Now, what are you going to focus on?

1. I am going to focus on getting all my work done in a high-quality manner, ahead of schedule. That way, I can feel the rewards of a focused effort.

2. With this gift of focus, I'm going to evaluate how I'm using my principles to recognize my values in my daily life.

3. My focus will help my discipline work for me, which will lead to an excellent, everlasting connection with my intuition.

Which one of those three thoughts is your preferred choice? Think to yourself: "Okay, I'll admit it." It's actually a trick question. They're all important, and it takes focus to do all three. So go the distance!

If you could always have 100% focus on one thing in your work environment, what would it be?

_____

Why?

_____

How would this type of discipline feel internally?

_____

How would it show externally?

_____

What could this focus potentially lead to?

_____

If you were going to focus on how you could use your principles to recognize your values, what value would you choose first?

_____

Why?

_____

How would this type of discipline feel internally?

_____

How would it show externally?

_____

What could this focus potentially lead to?

_____

What do you see as the largest benefit of utilizing your focus, in order to achieve a stronger sense of intuition?

_____

Why?

_____

How would this type of discipline feel internally?

_____

How would it show externally?

_____

What could this focus potentially lead to?

_____

What are three benefits you're going to receive by gaining a stronger sense of discipline that's purpose-driven and exciting?

1. _____
2. _____
3. _____

Congratulations on completing the sixth step of your bridge to intuition. You're so close to knowing the values you need in order to live a 3 Second Rule way of life. In fact, you're 2/3 of the way there!

CHAPTER EIGHT

Evaluation

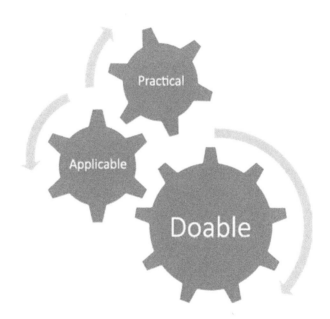

Have you heard the classic Michael Jackson song "Man in the Mirror"? It's about making the world a better place, by first making a change in yourself. This sentiment is completely true. In order to make a change in your life, what do you think you need to do first? Evaluate, of course! Changing without evaluating is like putting the cart before the horse. I'm confident about this: You've already grown exponentially by reading this book, so you understand that such an act would go 100% against your intuition. Why head off to the races and leave your vehicle behind, right?

When it comes to evaluating your progress, you need to do a few specific things. First, you need to decide what your evaluation will be based on. The legwork comes before the implementation. Here's what you'll need to do:

- ✓ Establish clearly defined expectations.
- ✓ List the steps to achieve your goal.
- ✓ Know the purpose behind your goal.
- ✓ Know you can make the necessary effort.
- ✓ Be reasonable.
- ✓ Be practical, and make sure you can adhere to your time commitments.
- ✓ Find a state of being that means this: Working on what you wish to evaluate is as necessary as breathing.
- ✓ Challenge yourself.

These basic ground rules really help you get in an evaluative state of mind. When you evaluate, you're brought back to that "man in the mirror." What are you willing to accept seeing on evaluation day?

With the criteria for the legwork and implementation in place, here's a list of what a good self-evaluation has the potential to become:

- ✓ It's an effective tool to gauge where you are, compared to your expectations. Then you can see where you'll excel, and where you'll struggle.
- ✓ Breaking it down even further, you give yourself the potential to really pinpoint your strengths and weaknesses.
- ✓ It's a great way to find out if you've really picked the proper things to be passionate about. If you aren't connected with your purpose, your action (or lack of it) will reveal it.
- ✓ When you've set big goals for big aspirations, you often overreach what's truly feasible. Perhaps practicality shuns you, and your overly ambitious desire sets you up for failure. If so, don't surrender. Take this information as a message to fine-tune and tweak your goal. As they say, Rome wasn't built in a day. Likewise, intuition wasn't mastered in a minute.
- ✓ Rationality is often underestimated, but it's an ideal way to ensure that you can remain on a positive track. If you make unrealistic expectations and demands on yourself, it trickles down into a festering pool of "icky stuff." We'll leave the rest to your imagination.
- ✓ If you need to gain self-confidence to achieve your intuitive goal, don't expect that it will happen just because you want it to. Accept that it'll take time, new thought patterns, and all the

other supporting actions that will allow you to go the distance.

✓ Live in a state of being that involves channeling feelings of success in your daily life. This simple activity can seem odd at first, but ultimately, it ends up making your "I can do it" attitude do a lot of the work for you.

✓ George S. Patton said, "Accept the challenges, so that you can feel the exhilaration of victory." Therefore, be bold and ambitious about the challenges you present for yourself, but also realize that the definition of the word "challenge" does not include "setting yourself up for failure."

Remember, the way you evaluate your actions really shows you the big picture of what you're doing. It also allows you to see if you're in control of the following:

✓ Taking practical actions to help you succeed.

✓ Prioritizing the state of being that you've set out to accomplish.

✓ Knowing how aware you are of your own personality traits. Are you ambitious, while still being focused on achieving what's doable? Here's an example of something that's not doable for me: Being the starting center for the Cavs. Well...maybe....

Are you ready to evaluate? I felt a resounding yes, which is great, because I'm ready to give you the three building blocks that lead to becoming an expert at self-evaluation.

Practice Being Practical

Being practical is not glamorous, but in the face of glitz, it is gutsy! Admit it: When you think about practical people, you probably think of individuals who don't dream big or pursue what they want with vigor and passion. I'm going to put the sizzle in the word "practical" by showing you the following:

- ✓ What it is: You've got to know in order to grow!
- ✓ How it benefits you: Everyone loves to benefit, right?
- ✓ Why you'll love it: We'd all prefer to love something than dread it.

A Story About Practicing Patience

There once was a guy named Dalton, who was completely obsessed with efficiency. He was a construction worker and loved to be the first one done with everything. He made every effort possible to keep his deadlines. Keep in mind that these deadlines were imposed by him. He was just so competitive that he couldn't resist them. He believed that he'd get to go home early, that he would impress people, and that he would be promoted first.

A guy named Patrick was in the exact same job. Patrick did not move at Dalton's rapid pace. He preferred to be more methodical. He put thought into everything he did, and he made sure that it was done precisely to every specification, even if it meant he had to do extra work to get the job done right.

One day, Dalton and Patrick's supervisor came up to them and said, "We've got to put up all the sheetrock in this office today." At first, the construction workers agreed that it wouldn't be a problem. Then Patrick realized that they didn't have enough sheetrock with the right thickness. So he went to his supervisor and told him about it. The supervisor thanked him, called in an order, and instructed Patrick to go pick it up.

But Dalton didn't want anything to do with that: He wasn't going to sit around and do nothing all day. That would require patience that he did not have. Even though the sheetrock was an entire 1/8" too thick, he looked at it and thought, "No one will notice the difference." Then he got to work, putting up sheet after sheet. He was fast and efficient, and he thought it looked great. Just as he put up the last sheet, Patrick returned with the correct sheetrock, and the two unloaded it to start finishing the room.

"Wow, you got a lot done," Patrick said.

"Yup," Dalton replied. "Now we'll both be done early tonight."

When Patrick turned his back for a second, Dalton got back to work. He started putting up the new sheetrock, so he could finish the project. As he put the first sheet up, the supervisor came over and mumbled, "What the..." Then he walked over to the new sheet of drywall, and back at the other sheets that were already up. There was a difference in height of approximately 1/8". "Did you put up the wrong sheetrock?"

"Yes," Dalton said. He didn't even think twice about it, and reached for another sheet.

"Stop," the supervisor said. He was struggling to stay calm. "Do you notice anything strange?" he asked Dalton. The supervisor's eyes darted from sheet to sheet.

Now, Dalton wasn't stupid, and there was no way that he could play dumb about that 1/8" difference. "Oops, how about I put up a strip of wood? No one will ever know the difference then," he said, trying to sound optimistic.

"I'll know. You'll know. And it would be foolish to think the customer wouldn't, right?" the supervisor said, staring Dalton in the eyes.

"Well, what can I do? It's all done now. It wouldn't be practical to take it down. Maybe we should just go back and replace the other sheetrock."

"We? Would that be a practical use of my time? Of Patrick's time?" the supervisor calmly asked.

Dalton didn't want to say it because he was feeling stubborn, but he grumbled, "No."

"Okay then. Why don't you work on taking down that sheetrock you put up? Patrick can start on the other side, and work his way toward you. Then at the end of the day, you can just stay and finish the job, okay?"

Dalton didn't think it was okay, but he had no choice.

That night, Dalton ended up putting in a bunch of extra hours of work, which caused him to miss the draft party for his fantasy football league. And he also lost some credibility with his boss, all because he was impatient and impractical. Would he like it if someone did the same thing in his home? Probably not.

Lesson learned. Being practical ultimately saves time, money, and (in some cases) dignity.

If practicality doesn't come naturally to you, why not practice it? It makes sense, since this is a practical world, where practical actions lead to success. Below are five ways to become more practical. You can achieve these goals!

1. **Learn to cope.**
   Practical people know how to deal with problems without freaking out. They don't whine, delay, or blame others. They take care of what they need to. What does this tactic mean for you? Once you're connected to your intuition, this goal will be considerably easier to achieve. Then you'll gain a clearer, faster picture.

2. <u>Take responsibility, and be responsible.</u>

Responsibility requires acceptance. In order to take responsibility when you need to, you MUST accept what's happening in your life. However, taking responsibility for something that's not your fault goes against every grain of common sense and intuition. And this situation causes you to teeter over the line into martyrdom, so try to avoid it!

3. <u>Know your options.</u>

Every problem has a solution. Depending on what the problem is, practical people can evaluate the options through a balance of logic and emotion. The more self-aware you are, the easier it is to evaluate solutions that are practical, strategic, and effective.

4. <u>Embrace some good old-fashioned common sense and problem-solving.</u>

One of the best gifts of practicality is the ability to boil everything down to the facts. This tactic prevents wasted time and energy. Instead of going off on a tangent or getting obsessed with small details, you can use that time to get a sense of the big picture. In this capacity, intuition is also very effective. If you sense that something isn't important, it probably isn't. Remember, if you're not a forensic scientist, you likely don't have to worry about the small nuances that piece the big puzzle together, especially not when you're "in the moment."

5. **Make sure that your self-esteem is intact.**

    In order to walk the talk, your inner dialogue has to be as confident as your external attitude. Smart solutions and good ideas are not always popular. However, you're putting yourself in a good spot if you can confidently relay a good message, and show why your suggestion is both practical and applicable. Remember the mirror: Who do you see looking back at you?

In all of life's pursuits, practicing being practical is quite a relief. In the end, it actually allows you to be more creative, dynamic, and bold in everything you do. It's not a coincidence that those same benefits are the byproducts of good, reliable intuition.

The Applicable State of Being

Consider what you'd say if someone asked you whether or not you know how to live in the moment. Would you be able to evaluate it, without making assumptions that are based on preconceived notions? If your answer was that you could just freeze the moment and discard any past inferences, you'd be wrong. This tactic cannot be accomplished, no matter how hard you try. But here's the confusing part: It's still necessary to try!

The way to effectively evaluate a situation is to live in a state of being. This state is a combination of the following:

✓   Intuition

- ✓ Self-confidence
- ✓ The processing of logical thoughts
- ✓ Mindfulness

And when done properly, this combination all happens within a 3-second timespan.

Below is an example of how this state of being can work effectively. It's rooted in the hope that many parents have for their children when they turn into young adults. For a moment, put yourself in the shoes of this parent:

You've done your part and explained why your children need to resist drugs and alcohol. Safer choices. Fewer risks of addictive behaviors. Drugs are destructive to future goals. You've had some great conversations about these topics, and you really believe that your message got through.

But...

There's still that flicker of doubt. You understand peer pressure. After all, you were a kid once, and you made your fair share of mistakes. And to see for yourself, you ignored your parent's advice. Still, you have to let them try.

Now your daughter is with a group of friends. The guy she's crushing on is paying attention to her, drinking some beer, and having fun. "Do you want one?" he asks.

Her wheels are turning, evaluating it all. The crush. But she's driving later. Your words. Her ability to stand strong. But dang, it's so much harder to resist in real life than it was in the fictional scenario that she discussed with you.

A lot is riding on this moment...

"No, that's okay," she says with a smile. Then she braces herself to be rejected or called a geek.

"You sure?" he asks.

She just nods her head.

"Okay, cool." That's what he says. Then maybe he stays, or maybe he moves on. But guess what persevered? Your hard work! It wasn't just talk. It also became applicable!

An applicable state of being is the sweet spot. In it, two concepts meet: What we've been taught, and what we sense is the right thing. In this example, it took a bit more than 3 seconds to do the right thing, but it's still a monumental victory.

As you proceed along your journey to mastering your best intuitive decision-making, I encourage you to take the approach of a teenager learning and growing into themselves.

Here are some guiding questions to help you out. They're short, precise, and easy to remember:

- ✓ Does this choice go against my principles?
- ✓ Does it feel like a smart choice?
- ✓ Will it seem like it was a good idea tomorrow?

For most people, the chance of truly experiencing a moment when you have to make a massive decision within a few seconds is very slim. These "opportunities of a lifetime" aren't really that common — despite what people say! Just know that someone else's desire to immediately have something happen for them doesn't have to involve you. It may be tough to accept, but please know this: Just because someone else desperately wants something in a given moment, that doesn't mean that you have to give it to them. If it isn't right for you, always be mindful of that. What about what you want and need? That matters, too!

Here's what I've learned: The more comfortable you are at making decisions based on what's best for you, the better the outcome will be. More often than not, you'll find the following:

- ✓ The person asking will understand.
- ✓ You'll be able to help someone else come up with a better, more applicable solution.
- ✓ People will admire and respect you when you make quick, decisive choices.
- ✓ You earn more respect.

Perhaps you're still thinking, "Man, I don't really know about that. Easier said than done." If so, consider this alternate scenario:

You manage to say you have to think about it. What can they do but agree with you, right? The entire time you're thinking about it, your subconscious and conscious minds are saying it's not a good idea. So just say no. Why go through a debate, and give someone else hope that you'll seriously consider something, just for appearances' sake? When that person asks why you won't even think about it (and they will), tell them that!

The power of application will revolutionize your mind!

It's Always Doable

You have to evaluate your plans to know how achievable they are. And you know, it's the damnedest thing: There are times when a goal seems completely achievable. But when you're in the swing of things, you end up struggling with it. It's not nearly as easy as you thought. It's like losing that last five pounds. For some inexplicable reason, there's resistance.

When you find yourself having your day in the sun with your goal, it's time to explore the 5 W's and an H from journalism:

- ✓ **W**ho is standing in the way of this goal actually being doable?
- ✓ **W**hat can be done to make the goal doable?

✓ Where will your goal manifest itself?
✓ When should you expect results from your shift of strategy?
✓ Why will the goal be more doable after you do research and tweak it?
✓ How can you tap into new resources?

A complicated, grueling two-day process isn't necessary to know if something is doable. All you need to do is instinctually evaluate the situation. And what a relief that is. No more pretending, no more pondering, no more hassles. Imagine how much more time you would have if you followed this process.

Take some time to imagine what it's like to actually succeed at doing something you set out to do. Remember those feelings. Maybe it was when you finally earned your degree. Perhaps it was your first paycheck. It could be anything, but you felt a sense of pride (an inner voice you couldn't ignore) shouting, "Yes, I did it. I knew I could!"

The truth is that we often stop ourselves from making something doable in our lives. When we stop getting in our own way, we'll be able to align ourselves with powerful, impactful, intuitive decisions. Keep in mind that the big decisions aren't the only ones that dictate the flow of our lives; the small ones do as well. If you evaluate what is practical, doable, and applicable to you, it helps you see these decisions with greater clarity.

Activating Your Evaluation

Evaluation can either be simple or complicated. Which option do you choose? To find the most practical solutions, would you rather study intensively, begin researching the applications that the solution would have in your life, decide that the goal is doable, and pursue the goal until it's time to reevaluate? Whew... is your head spinning? Or would you rather find a practical way to develop strategies that will help you achieve your goals? If you didn't choose the latter option, please go back to the beginning of the book, and start reading again! We all have different starting points, after all.

The 3 Second Rule takes you from an unnecessarily complicated thought process to a streamlined, logical one. With the 3 Second Rule, you can get straight to the message, and not get bogged down by clutter. Mental housecleaning is at the heart of the rule. By mentally cleaning house, you will be able to decisively and accurately make decisions in a fraction of the time that it used to take you. Yes!

Make this list your 1, 2, 3 for evaluating everything:

1. Is it practical?
2. Is it applicable?
3. Is it doable?

The Practicality Manifesto

Really, being practical is being brilliant. It's the most effective way to sift through the drama of too many emotions or the starkness of solid, factual evidence. It's a perfect blend: When paired with intuition, it's as amazing as pairing a robust red wine with a Kobe steak. Divine.

Now let's get down to the nitty-gritty. To find out how practical you really are, ask yourself the following questions:

- ✓ When you look at two people in conflict, are you able to see a resolution that they're clueless of?
- ✓ You have a big, bold idea for work, and someone instantly dismisses it. What do you do? Accept their rejection, or present the practical, logical case for your idea? Why?
- ✓ You just got a $100 bonus. Do you use it for fun? (After all, it wasn't expected.) Or do you make a payment on a bill, or put it into savings? What spurs your decision? (Keep in mind that there really isn't a right or wrong answer. But also keep in mind that it isn't really practical to spend the money on fun when you're struggling to pay your bills. On the other hand, it might be a great mental break, and a way to rejuvenate you.)
- ✓ How do you respond to the dreamers you run across? Do you think they're foolish and unwise, or are you envious of them?

- ✓ Do you have confidence in the way that you evaluate situations? Why or why not?
- ✓ If you follow someone's lead and step out of your comfort zone to take their approach to solving a problem, how does that feel? Exciting? Nerve-wracking? Unnatural?
- ✓ Would you feel more confident about using practicality in your life if you had more self-esteem?
- ✓ Are you evaluating strategies to increase your comfort with practicality?
- ✓ How do you view the word "practicality"?

What is your ideal definition of the practicality that you'd like to see in your life? Define a practical version of yourself!

_____

_____

_____

Write down how you envision feeling — emotionally, mentally, and even physically — after using a precise, practical approach to solving a problem. Think about everything you might change for the better, including your stress levels and your lifestyle.

_____

_____

_____

What are three benefits you believe will happen in your life as you become comfortable with being practical?

1. _____
2. _____
3. _____

Having higher self-esteem is a large part of practicality. When people have low self-esteem, they're afraid to veer off-course, and do what they instinctually know is best. How is your self-esteem level at this moment? Is it level enough to start making your evaluation strategies more practical? Why?

_____
_____
_____
_____

Now let's affirm the wonderful benefits of practicality. Whether or not you use these affirmations is up to you. But unless you'd deem yourself more than 95% practical, you may want to memorize a few of them:

- ✓ When I'm practical, I can reach for the stars.
- ✓ Practical evaluation helps me reduce stress levels.
- ✓ Respect is earned through practical evaluation.
- ✓ Being more practical is a good thing.
- ✓ By being practical, I'm more attuned to my intuition.

Can you think of any other power statements that you could use to embrace being practical? You should wear your practicality like a badge of honor. Don't think poorly of it: Remember that it can make a wonderful difference in how you evaluate everything!

The Art of Application

Do you know who Barry White was? He's the R&B singer with a deep, silky voice. In fact, if you know what he sounds like, I'll bet you're hearing this paragraph in his voice. White was exceptional at using that voice to convey many messages about life. You may not have a voice like that, but you do have the skills to evaluate everything in your life with greater ease and confidence.

How can you use both your natural and developed gifts to apply the 3 Second Rule to your life? Look at these generalizations, in order to help you find the best ways to connect with your intuition:

- ✓ You're listening to a disagreement, and you're able to dissect the valid points of both arguments, while discrediting the purely emotional words.
- ✓ If you have the ability to remain focused on what the real problem is, it will help you evaluate the important matters, rather than the extraneous tangents.
- ✓ Others will come to you for wisdom about how to manage and embrace change.
- ✓ You remain calm when you explain your strategies, find ways to show that you're firm in

your thoughts, and help others better understand your solutions.

What do you believe are your most useful, natural skills while evaluating decisions?

_____

_____

_____

_____

What are some weaknesses that lessen your ability to quickly and accurately evaluate situations? (Example: Not being able to say no.)

_____

_____

_____

_____

How can you use your strengths to reduce or eliminate your weaknesses?

_____

_____

_____

_____

Are you willing to commit to using practicality, so you can better evaluate all aspects of your life?
1. Yes
2. No

Name one thing in your life that you're in the process of evaluating right now. Maybe it's related to your relationships, finances, or career.

_____

_____

_____

Remember, if your goal involves other people, you can't force them to do anything they don't want to do. The only things you can control are your engagement and effort. Recall what you've attempted in the past, and stay in a practical state of mind. What's a new, uncomplicated idea that you can try?

_____

_____

_____

Explain the role of intuition in this new idea. How much is involved?

_____

_____

_____

By now, you should be excited about being a practical person. Let's face it: We all like to succeed. When you're about to evaluate a situation, make note of what didn't work, and commit that information to memory. This process feeds your intuitive thought process. Then there's nothing you can't do!

Do-Do-Doable

Newsflash: You cannot say something isn't doable unless you make a concerted effort to do it first! This section is all about the importance of action. It's a thought process that involves the literal action that's necessary for making something happen.

Perhaps your goal is to get into great physical shape. If so, you can read all the books in the world, but if you don't actually do something physical, it isn't going to happen. On the flipside, perhaps your goal is to write a book about fitness. If all you do is exercise, play, and move, you aren't going to get very far with that book, are you? When you ask what's doable, be mindful of these differences.

Think about something you wanted to accomplish but haven't. Write it down.

_____

_____

_____

Was this goal actually doable? If not, why?

_____

_____

_____

If it wasn't doable, write down something else that you wanted to accomplish — which is doable, but that you haven't achieved.

_____

_____

_____

Let's use this goal as your starting point. We're going to assume that this goal is something you want to accomplish.

What are three things you can do today to accomplish what you'd like to do?

1. _____

2. _____

3. _____

Create a vision of how this accomplishment will play out, and think of three things you're going to do to achieve it. Be as descriptive as possible!

1. _____

2. _____

3. _____

Describe the role your intuition played in creating your vision.

_____

_____

_____

Did you rely on your intuition enough? If yes, how so? If no, why not?

_____

_____

_____

How could you achieve your goal without using intuitive instincts?

_____

_____

_____

In what way will intuition be a better guide for you?

_____

_____

_____

Think about everything you've read in this chapter about proper evaluation. In your evaluation strategy below, you'll write down some generalized strengths.

When being practical, my strengths are:

_____

_____

When taking applicable actions, my strengths are:

_____

_____

When focusing on what's doable, my strengths are:

_____

_____

You've got this. With all the information you've gleaned from this book and the high level of awareness that makes you an elite thinker, your intuition is going to receive all the positive energy and fuel you can imagine.

Things are going to happen, and they're going to be great!

Congratulations on completing the seventh step of evaluation. It's so exciting, and guess what? You only have one more block left before your bridge is built. After that, the fruits of your intuition will begin manifesting themselves. So be prepared: It's time to recognize the fulfillment in achievement! This recognition involves a celebration of your improvements and strengths.

CHAPTER NINE

Fulfillment

Sometimes, it's easier to define what fulfillment is *not* than what it *is*. It is not having the most expensive things, or giving everyone the impression that your life is perfect in every way. I'm not saying that everyone who gives off that impression is full of it, but let's get real: People are people, regardless of social status. So wealthy people have problems, too. Money doesn't dictate self-worth, work ethic, or integrity. And it certainly doesn't guarantee an engaged, beneficial level of intuition.

So what does fulfillment feel like?

Over the years, I've posed this question to a number of people, and they shared what they think fulfillment feels like:

- ✓ A natural state
- ✓ A warm, fuzzy feeling
- ✓ Excitement
- ✓ Control
- ✓ Happiness in career
- ✓ Happiness in life
- ✓ Acceptance of oneself
- ✓ A great dinner
- ✓ Appreciation
- ✓ A recognition of blessings
- ✓ Success
- ✓ The desire to achieve something more

These answers tell me that fulfillment means something different for everyone. It's based on their expectations, the effort they put into life, and the way they choose to view the rewards of their actions.

It's possible to have different levels of fulfillment in different areas of our lives. For example, a stay-at-home mom may experience incredible fulfillment. However, she may still have the desire to achieve things in the vocational world. Likewise, a working woman may love her career and find it fulfilling. But she also recognizes that it would be great to more frequently be around during the day for her little ones.

What does this dichotomy say? To me, it says that fulfillment comes from balance. We don't have to compromise in our lives, but we do have to understand exactly what allows us to experience fulfillment, however we define it. To accomplish this fulfillment, here's what we require:

- ✓ An idea of what our emotional rewards are.
- ✓ A solid vision of what fulfillment feels like.
- ✓ A feeling of peace about the choices we've made in life.

I want you to be mindful of one aspect of fulfillment: It cannot be attached to a big bank account. Fulfillment makes you internally wealthy. And depending on how well you're using your intuition, it could lead to the big bucks. But that's the bonus, not the real prize.

Here's one last thing I really want you to remember about fulfillment: its potential to help define your life. Fulfillment allows you to recognize how thankful you can be, and just how far you've come. It's inspiring to feel gratitude for your efforts, as well as your ability to recognize what needs to change in your life. Once you go through all the stages in this book, you'll know yourself better than most. You may not be able to explain it, but you'll intuitively know it!

Reaping Your Earned Rewards

People have different reactions to reaping the rewards of their hard work and actions. Here are some of the reactions I've seen over the years:

- ✓ *You get so excited that you ride that reward, and forget about the needs in the rest of your life.* For example, you work really hard and earn your largest commission check ever. Then you start slacking off. Before you know it, your pipeline is dwindling, and you're playing catch-up.
- ✓ *You pretend there was no reward, because you have too much to do.* Maybe you don't even feel like you deserve it. For example, you have a record commission check, and won't even shell out enough to take your wife out for a celebration dinner. After all, your long hours and hard work have impacted her, too!
- ✓ *You earn that reward and recognize it as being exciting.* You even share the news with people you care about. But then you get back to work, and you use the reward to create further drive, which helps you continue pursuing your goals. For example, you get the commission check, take your spouse out to dinner, and think about what you learned while you were getting that reward. You then use that information to duplicate your

success, perhaps faster and more effectively. You add this experience to your intuitive thought, and let your intuition work for you!

It's my greatest hope that the third option is the way you'll react to achieving rewards.

It's not easy to get to the point in life where you find fulfillment through receiving authentic rewards. It takes hard work. What do you think about the power of hard work? Here are a few interesting statistics that were uncovered in a survey about it:

- ✓ 54% of males believe in the power of hard work.
- ✓ 59.2% of females believe in it.[20]

Are you as surprised as me that more people don't believe in hard work? You might think it's a matter of age, but check out this next set of statistics:

- ✓ 60% of people between the ages of 18 and 29 believe in the power of hard work.
- ✓ 57.8% of people between the ages of 30 and 44 believe in it.
- ✓ 55.5% people between the ages of 45 and 64 believe in it.
- ✓ 53% of people 65 years old or older believe in it.

Maybe we've been a bit too hard on millennials! They seem to embrace hard work as much as the rest of us.

---

[20]Belief in Hard Work Survey. Statistic Brain. March 4, 2016.
http://www.statisticbrain.com/percent-who-believe-in-the-power-of-hard-work/.

Perhaps it's just our natural instinct to gravitate toward the negative, rather than the positive.

By becoming fulfilled and recognizing your rewards, you can remember to focus more on the positive. And that will make a positive difference!

Do you know what happens to us when we work hard to achieve something we want, and actually start succeeding at it? Our emotions shift, and give us some interesting side benefits, including:

- ✓ **A feeling of autonomy:** A desire to direct our own lives, and not have our experiences and outcomes be dictated by others.
- ✓ **A sense of mastery:** Once we know we can get better at things, we long to keep getting better at them.
- ✓ **A desire for purpose:** When we understand why we're doing something, we're more purposeful and intentional in achieving it.

Remember, you can't lose your intuition when you incorporate the three benefits above. In addition, the rewards are more inspiring, and they're very seldom related to anything financial.

In fact, I came across a fantastic research study that emphasizes this point. In this world, money is necessary, but far too often, it can become your master. So it's good to know that some research shows that people are more motivated by emotions than money:

> "Psychologists Teresa Amabile and Steven Kramer interviewed over 600 managers and found a shocking result. 95% of managers misunderstood what motivates employees. They thought what motivates employees was making money, getting raises and bonuses. In fact, after analyzing over 12,000 employee diary entries, they discovered that the number one work motivator was emotion, not financial incentive: it's the feeling of making progress every day toward a meaningful goal. In fact, Dan Pink found that actually the exact opposite is true:

> *'The larger the monetary reward, the poorer the performance. Money doesn't motivate us at all. Instead, emotions do.'"* [21]

The article goes on to summarize an experiment by Dr. Edward Deci:

> "People were sitting in a room and tried to solve a puzzle while Deci measured how much time they put in, before giving up. For Group A, he offered a cash reward for successfully solving the puzzle, and as you might expect, those people spent almost twice as much

---

[21]"The Science Behind What Motivates Us to Get Up for Work Every Day." Chen, Walter. Last updated March 22, 2016. https://blog.bufferapp.com/the-science-of-what-motivates-us-to-get-up-for-work-every-day.

time trying to solve the puzzle as those people in Group B who weren't offered a prize.

A surprising thing happened the next day, when Deci told Group A that there wasn't enough money to pay them this time around: Group A lost interest in the puzzle. Group B, on the other hand, having never been offered money, worked on the puzzles longer and longer in each consecutive session and maintained a higher level of sustained interest than Group A."

Good to know!

What does this tell you? Hopefully, that money won't be the greatest reward you gain from using intuition to guide your life. If anything, money gives you one place *not* to look for a reward. And if you're having trouble deciding exactly where to look, put on your success goggles!

Success Goggles

Our success goggles are amazing, but if I could invent a pair that would do all the hard work for us, I wouldn't. You have to get to the point of looking at success as a journey that doesn't have shortcuts. Then you'll be able to tap into the rewards you dream of.

When your success goggles are on, you can look around and think, "How can I make the most out of this situation? What lesson can I learn? What's my takeaway?" Everything we see, say, or do matters. Our minds are like supercomputers: (Ironically) performing more functions in a given second than we can fathom. So it's important to find the takeaway from a situation, and store it as a reference point. Our success goggles are intricately linked to our intuitions.

Success goggles also help us internally improve by assisting with the self-care of our hearts, souls, and emotions. Are you wondering how emotions can be successful? Let me explain...

We cannot control that we have certain emotions — even at the strangest times. They just occur, so trying to resist them or run away is silly. But once someone is wearing their success goggles, shockingly negative emotions can be diffused. Then they won't explode on us, and create trouble where there wasn't any.

For example, you go to surprise your girlfriend at work. But you end up being the one surprised. She's talking to some guy, and they're laughing, being carefree, and having fun. You instantly wonder who the guy is. What's going on? Is he making a move? You are jealous! Then she looks at you with the smile you fell in love with. So you walk over, meet the guy, and see a ring on his hand.

After analyzing this kind of experience, you can learn to examine the source of surprising, negative emotions. In the scenario above, you can see that these emotions were going on in your head, and no one else's. When your success goggles are on, you learn from those experiences and lessen your risk of overreacting. With emotions such as jealousy, your success goggles can save you a lot of embarrassment and recovery time.

As your intuition homes in, make sure you're charging your success goggles. With them, you can experience the following:

- ✓ The awareness to see the results of your efforts
- ✓ Empathy for others, instead of judgment
- ✓ A higher level of happiness
- ✓ Lower stress levels
- ✓ Greater problem-solving capabilities
- ✓ More clarity about what's important to you
- ✓ A better understanding about what your reactions are
- ✓ Fewer situations that involve you acting out in a counterproductive manner
- ✓ More opportunities to do fantastic things
- ✓ Success in your career
- ✓ Success in your personal relationships
- ✓ The opportunity to mentor others
- ✓ The ability to inspire

The Fable of Hercules and the Waggoner

After a heavy rain, a farmer was driving his wagon along a muddy country road. The horses could hardly drag the load through the deep mud. Then when one of the wheels sank into a rut, it finally came to a standstill.

The farmer climbed down from his seat, stood beside the wagon, and looked at it. But he made no effort to get it out of the rut. All he did was curse his bad luck, and loudly call on Hercules to come to his aid. Then Hercules actually appeared, and said:

"Put your shoulder to the wheel, man, and urge your horses on. Do you think you can move the wagon by simply looking at it and whining about it? Hercules will not help you unless you make some effort to help yourself."

And when the farmer put his shoulder to the wheel and urged the horses, the wagon moved very readily. And soon, the farmer was riding along, very content about the lesson he'd learned. [22]

Good lessons are helpful for us, and great ways to learn to use our success goggles. Then we will help both ourselves and others!

Finding Your Piece of Peace

Have you ever attached your hope for inner peace to what's happening in the world around you? If you have, you've set yourself up for a great disservice. As your intuition develops, you'll be able to more fully recognize this fact.

When we seek inner peace, we can obtain a great many things, including the following:

---

[22]"Business Fables, Fairytales, Stories, and Management Lessons". August 4, 2007. http://fairy-tales-fables-business.blogspot.com/2007/08/self-help-perseverance-and-success.html.

- ✓ An increased sense of faith
- ✓ Enhanced wellbeing
- ✓ An understanding of the impact your actions have on you
- ✓ The essentials of happiness
- ✓ Greater value at work
- ✓ Stronger connections in your personal life
- ✓ A greater understanding of your impact on your world and environment
- ✓ Contentment when you're alone

Seeking inner peace is something that has been prevalent for all time, and it tells us two things for certain:

- ✓ People want it.
- ✓ People achieve it.

Some of the greatest masters of all time shared insight and wisdom with us about the benefits and possibilities of achieving inner peace. Below are a few personal favorites. Of course, the first step is living in an aware and intuitive state of existence.

Mahatma Gandhi said, "Nobody can hurt me without my permission." By remembering this statement, you can always find solutions without losing your inner peace. (At least you won't lose it for long.)

Renowned philosopher and Father of Taoism, Lao Tzu, said, "The best fighter is never angry." This statement is a reminder that we can gain control of negative emotions through inner peace. So we are very capable of solving painful and intense problems without having to be angered by them first.

Henry Fielding, a novelist from the UK, shared: "I am content; that is a blessing greater than riches; and he to whom that is given need ask no more." This statement is a wonderful reminder that our greatest wealth comes from the inside out, so it's an abundance of self-worth and positivity.

Born in 567 BC, Gautama Buddha is credited with saying, "Peace comes from within. Do not seek it without." See, what I've shared with you about the 3 Second Rule isn't farfetched at all; if it's right by Buddha, it's pretty solid.

Rainer Maria Rilke was a Bohemian-Austrian poet who penned, "Have patience with everything that remains unsolved in your heart...live in the question." Inner peace encourages us not to force outcomes, but to allow our intuition to guide us to the answers when we're ready to hear them.

Elizabeth Gilbert, author of a book about her journey to self-discovery and healing, wrote, "We don't realize that, somewhere within us all, there does exist a supreme self who is eternally at peace." This statement tells me (and hopefully tells you) that we all have the potential to experience inner peace, if we allow ourselves to.

Dalai Lama XIV expresses a message of forgiveness to show us the promise of inner peace. He says, "We can never obtain peace in the outer world until we make peace with ourselves." Forgive, grow, and go!

Bohdi Sanders, a martial artist, author, and lifelong student of wisdom, wrote: "Never respond to an angry person with a fiery comeback, even if he deserves it... Don't allow his anger to become your anger." This statement is an excellent reminder that we are all in control of what we choose to do with our lives, including embracing our intuition.

Ralph Waldo Emerson is an author who has given us great bits of wisdom and insight. Regarding inner peace, he wrote, "Nothing external to you has any power over you." This statement represents an excellent reminder that we should never give our personal energy and inner wellbeing to anyone or anything else.

Thought leader Eckhart Tolle reminds us: "Pleasure is always derived from something outside you, whereas joy arises from within." This quote reiterates the message I've tried to relay to you (hopefully successfully) that before anything else can bring us lasting joy and blessings, we must first have our internal house in order, which means that our instincts should be operating at a high level.

Practice may not make perfect, but it does create the habits that allow you to master your greatest desires, including a connection with your intuition. Therefore, for a parting thought on inner peace, I can think of no one better than author Roy T. Bennett: "When you do the right thing, you get the feeling of peace and serenity associated with it. Do it again and again."

Activating Your Fulfillment

"O fulfillment, fulfillment, wherefore art thou, fulfillment?" That's my riff on Shakespeare for the 3 Second Rule. You shouldn't *consciously* seek fulfillment. Instead, tap into all the things you've learned in this book. They will take you to the place of fulfillment, even if you don't completely realize it. It's quite brilliant, actually.

Let's start by walking through what we've learned so far. Just as each step helps you build a bridge to intuition, it also brings you a step closer to fulfillment.

Answer each of these questions about intuition:

Here's how I define intuition:

_____

_____

Here's how I use intuition:

_____

_____

Here's how I feel about intuition:

_____

_____

Here's how I can actively seek intuition:

_____

_____

I will avoid being passive about intuition by:

_____

_____

I will not allow myself to fear my intuition by:

_____

_____

I can gain confidence in my intuition by:

_____

_____

I now better understand intuition because:

_____

_____

I have a goal of developing intuition, so I can:

_____

_____

A feeling of excitement about intuition is surfacing in me because:

_____

_____

It's easy to feel energetic about intuition because:

_____

_____

I am ambitious about developing my intuition because:

_____

_____

Resilience is important to my intuition because it helps me:

_____

_____

By being alert, my intuition will:

_____

_____

My motivation about my intuition stems from:

_____

_____

The principles that will help my intuition flourish are:

_____

_____

My values rely on intuition because:

_____

_____

The most exciting reason to focus on intuition is:

_____

_____

Practically speaking, intuition will help me:

_____

_____

In my life, developing intuition will be most beneficial for:

_____

_____

Regarding intuition, here's my plan:

_____

_____

Now you're up to speed, so you're ready to tap into your fulfillment plans, according to the guidelines of the 3 Second Rule.

The Importance of a Reward System

When we work hard and put forth our best effort, it's important to reward ourselves in the right way. What is the right way? For starters, it doesn't contradict what you worked so hard to achieve. As long as you follow the guidelines and are not rewarding yourself in a counterproductive way, your potential is endless. Some rewards can be material, but remember the quotes that the thought leaders made about inner peace.

Close your eyes for a second, and think about the word "reward." Get yourself in the mood to think about rewards. Now, contemplate these questions with your eyes wide open:

✓ For this question, eliminate all notions of materialism: What would your reward be for achieving your biggest goal or desire? Why? What long-term value would it bring you?

- ✓ What's the best reward you can think of that doesn't cost a penny?
- ✓ Do you feel guilty about rewarding yourself? Perhaps you have children. If you do something great, do you still put their needs first? For instance, maybe your daughter loves the zoo, but you loathe it. So do you use your reward to take her to the zoo, rather than doing something *you* love, such as going to the mall? If so, do you think this reward system is fair?
- ✓ Do you know people who are great at rewarding themselves? What do they do?
- ✓ Can you relax and unwind when you give yourself a reward? Why?
- ✓ Do you believe in the value of rewards? Why?

What types of rewards bring the most value to your life? Why?

_____

_____

_____

Write down what you will do to ensure that you are enjoying the rewards you earn. (Remember, it's possible not to enjoy rewards, if we resist them for any reason.)

_____

_____

_____

What are three benefits that you believe you will have in your life if you allow yourself to reward your successes?

1. _____
2. _____
3. _____

Describe your history of giving yourself rewards for things you've accomplished.

_____
_____
_____
_____

Would you change this history? Why or why not?

_____
_____
_____
_____

It's almost surreal that someone would have to affirm the value of rewarding themselves. But for some people, it is necessary. If you are one of these people, smile and laugh about it a bit. Then get to work, and eliminate the guilt that comes from rewarding yourself in meaningful ways. Try repeating these statements:

- ✓ I deserve to experience rewards.
- ✓ Giving myself a reward is like giving myself a thank you gift for achieving something important.
- ✓ I'm reaping a hard-earned reward.

Amp yourself up for the potential that a well-earned reward can bring to your life! It's worth it in many ways. Giving yourself a special treat is giving yourself the fuel to keep pursuing great things.

The Power of Visualization

Have you ever been burnt by something that didn't turn out the way you wanted? Maybe somebody said something to you, and you couldn't think of the perfect reply in the moment. Perhaps someone that you considered a friend stabbed you in the back. Maybe you angrily overreacted to a situation, instead of handling it with dignity. Whatever the situation was, you replay it in your mind afterward, but with a better outcome.

It's time to evaluate your vision, and see how to use intuition to save yourself from repeating a bad situation. This evaluation will help your success goggles know what you want to see in the future:

- ✓ Replay a time when you weren't proud of your behavior. Now replay it again, but imagine yourself successfully handling the situation. Afterward, think about how different each feeling was that the two conclusions created.
- ✓ Now think about a vision of your future. Picture yourself using intuition to help navigate a nonemergency situation (such as a car running a light in front of you). Imagine the results of your

intuitive decision, and the benefits that you will ultimately earn from it.

Why is it important for you to use visualizations to foresee successful outcomes?

_____

_____

_____

_____

Do you think your visions are useful for achieving success and developing intuition? Why or why not?

_____

_____

_____

_____

Do you need any strategies to enhance your ability to properly visualize? If so, what are they?

_____

_____

_____

_____

Are you willing to commit to using visions to help you understand what a successful outcome looks like?
1. Yes
2. No

Is there anything you're currently visualizing? If so, what is it?

_____

_____

_____

If you currently don't have anything that you can actively envision doing successfully, come up with something to envision that you could succeed at. Don't worry if you start small!

_____

_____

_____

_____

Why will you use this vision to help you experience the reward of achieving a goal? And what is the reward?

_____

_____

_____

YES! Your bridge is complete. Now it's time to experience the amazing feelings that come from achieving full-circle intuition.

By all means, this reward should excite you, motivate you, and guide you. You're constantly a work in progress!

CHAPTER TEN

Full-Circle Intuition

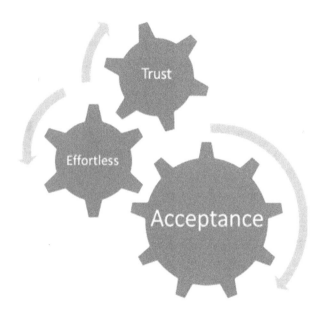

Welcome to the chapter focused on success. Here, you will find stories of individuals who have taken amazing strides toward having more intuition. I find this next chapter really exciting. If you're anything like me, you appreciate a good success story, especially when you understand all the work that goes into achieving it.

Intuition in Everyday Life

The Price

A woman was making her way into her house after work one day, and her neighbor called her over and asked if she'd consider selling her home. Since the woman and her husband had recently talked about selling it, she was a little surprised. She asked the neighbor how much he would offer for it. He gave her a very low number.

Caught off-guard, she smiled and said she'd talk to her husband about it. Obviously, it got her thinking. Had she and her husband overvalued their home? It didn't seem like they had. After a brief recap, he was quick to say, "No way." So they called a realtor, just to see what he had to say. Much to their surprise, they learned that their home was valued even higher than they'd thought. It turned out that the neighbor just wanted to get a good deal.

Without having the intuition that something was off, this couple might have assumed that their house wasn't worth that much, and sold it. Instead, by following their guts and doing a little research, they discovered that their neighbor was lacking integrity.

What a shame for the neighbor, but what a good thing for them to know!

Sensory Alert

Cameron was getting used to life at home without his son, who'd gone off to college on a football scholarship. He knew it was a big change, and that his son was busy. But he kept thinking that something was wrong. Nevertheless, he blew it off, believing that he was probably just struggling to adjust.

Yet the feelings persisted. And it didn't help that long, animated phone calls slowly turned into occasional texts and short, distracted conversations. Cameron finally asked his son if anything was wrong. As a reply, he received a somber, simple "No." So that text didn't make him feel any better.

After Cameron asked a few more times, he decided that it was only making him feel worse. He decided to go up and surprise his son on-campus. That way, he could look him in the eye and see what the deal was.

At first, his son was resistant, since he was caught off-guard. So Cameron said, "I can just sense that something is wrong. Why don't you tell me what it is, so we can figure it out?" Inside, he was trying not to overreact, and jump to the worst conclusions: drugs, depression...

Taking advantage of the moment, his son finally told him. He was struggling with maintaining his vigorous athletic schedule and his grades. As a result, he was in jeopardy of not being able to play the sport he loved.

Because of Cameron's intuition and his refusal to ignore the warning signs, he was able to help his son come up with a plan to save his football career, as well as his academic future!

Life's Close Calls

A mom was driving around town one day, picking her two kids up from their different schools. They were all getting ready to get some hard-earned ice cream as a promised treat.

She picked up her daughter from preschool first, secured her in her car seat, and drove over to the high school to pick up her son after track practice.

Afterward, they were waiting to turn right out of the high school parking lot. Then suddenly, an aggressive young driver whipped around her, and turned right directly in front of her, which forced her to put on her brakes. She was shaken and annoyed, warning her son in that typically maternal way: "You'd better never drive like that!" Then they kept going.

But that exact same car was stopped at the next light. When the light turned green, the car quickly took off. Bam! Another car ran the light, right into the side of the aggressive driver's car. The mother knew that they could have gotten hit if the aggressive driver hadn't cut them off.

Thankfully, the aggressive driver was more shaken up than hurt. But the mom couldn't help but look at the back seat and see her little one sitting there — safe in her seat, in the same spot where the car would have hit them.

What's the moral of this story? If we aren't quick to get annoyed at other people (even when the reason is valid), our intuition can help us put things in perspective. In the end, did the aggressive car really make them late for ice cream? Was it all going to be gone by the time they got there?

Don't Do It!

Ben was busy cleaning up his apartment, and getting ready for a date with his new girlfriend. He was eager to make a good impression. He wasn't a messy guy, but he knew she was a meticulously tidy woman. If he was going to be judged about anything, it would be the cleanliness of his place.

As he cleaned, he looked over to his collection of medieval weapons. They were replicas, but they were still heavy. Something about them had always appealed to him. He'd always wanted to hang a sword above the door, so he decided that he'd quickly do that.

When Ben retrieved his toolbox, he found that he didn't really have the right fastener, but he did find some thick screws. He believed that they'd be able to hold it up; he could always replace it later.

He was standing on his swiveling office chair, and reaching up to place the sword in the holder he'd just screwed in. At that moment, he heard a voice in his head say, "Don't do it."

He shook his head, shooing away the voice. He hung up the sword, and went to shower and get ready. Only a half-hour to spare!

Ben was in the kitchen preparing a few things for his date, when he heard a knock on the door. He smiled and called out, "Just a second!" Then there was one more knock.

Next, there was a crash.

The sword had fallen down. If Ben had been there just a second before, it would have fallen right on him or his date. That definitely would not have made a good impression!

Ben couldn't help but recall that voice in his head. Maybe ignoring it wasn't such a good idea.

This story is a great reminder of why we shouldn't ignore the voices that abruptly appear at unexpected times. It's our intuition pleading with us to reconsider what we're doing!

Intuition in the Business World

The Unexpected Meeting

When Cecily was preparing for a business trip, she had an unexpected thought about an old college friend named Amanda. It was so strange, and honestly, she couldn't remember the last time she'd thought about Amanda. She made a mental note to try and find a way to connect with her. She placed it with all her other mental notes about reaching out to someone.

Then she was off to the airport and onto her flight, which had a layover at Chicago O'Hare (the busiest airport in the US). With the delays, she missed her flight. In a huff, she went over to the VIP lounge to have a glass of wine and get some work done. Her best option was to pass the time by being productive.

She sat down at a small round table in the corner of the lounge, and instantly focused on what she had to do on her laptop.

"Oh my gosh, Cecily!"

Cecily jumped, startled out of her work trance. Her jaw dropped. Unbelievable. It was Amanda. She was floored, especially since Amanda had just popped into her mind that morning.

The two started talking, and that's when things got really interesting. Amanda was an executive recruiter, and she just happened to have a position open that was Cecily's dream job.

Can you guess where everything went from there?

The Numbers Don't Add Up

Ryan was the new CFO of a pretty big oil-refining company. Looking through the numbers, he saw that the amount of money they spent on electricity at one of their drill sites was staggering. He couldn't imagine how even the biggest machinery could produce a bill of $50,000 per month.

First, he checked the past records to look for any differences, but there were none. The only adjustments during the past two years were from differences in the yearly electricity rates.

Still not understanding it at all, Ryan began asking a few questions. But no one had a single answer. It was frustrating, but he was determined. For three solid weeks, he spent his free time mulling everything over, and trying to figure out why the past two years had led to such high bills. They hadn't installed any new equipment at any of the sites, and the site in question was actually logging fewer hours. Somehow, he sensed that the hours must have something to do with it.

Ryan began comparing what the bills were before and after the hours decreased. Then he took a trip to see the foreperson of the site and get a tour.

"This is the pump that handled the extra volume," the supervisor said.

"Is it still being used?" Ryan asked. The foreperson shook his head. So Ryan asked, "Why does it need to be turned on?" The foreperson said that no one had ever requested that it be turned off.

Ding! Ding! Ding!

By industry standards, the equipment was considered old. After Ryan turned it off, the amount of money saved each day was instantly noticeable. In the end, it saved the company nearly $20,000 per month.

As Ryan's case shows, having intuition is actually beneficial to businesses. As people come and go, questions often fall by the wayside. One curious, intuitive mind can make a substantial difference.

The Negotiation

Gail was in charge of finding new properties. Within the next few years, her employer was planning to move his growing business. She had a specific list of criteria, and made contact with a highly recommended leasing agent. Now it was time to go and take a look at a few properties.

Property #1 was pretty nice. It fit most of her criteria, but it was in a more expensive part of town. So it would be out of her price range by about 10%. She told the leasing agent that she'd keep it in mind.

Property #2 was an instant no-go because of the shady surrounding businesses and the crazy intersections with no lights.

Then she arrived at Property #3. It was exactly what she believed the business needed, and it fit all of Gail's criteria.

After consulting with the CEO and visiting the site, she was given the go-ahead to negotiate the lease. Gail was thrilled at how easy it had been to find the perfect property. Sadly, her happiness was short-lived.

The company that owned the building cited outlandish buildout requirements, upped the lease payments after they listed them, and asked for a more aggressive lease than the standard one.

They went back and forth. Finally, much to Gail's dismay, she had to swallow her pride and admit defeat. She went and shared the news with the CEO, who asked for other options. She mentioned the first building she'd looked at, and he wasn't appalled by the small difference in payments. When he looked at the building, he was immediately sold, seeing that the value of a better location was well worth the extra 10%.

Even though Gail was disappointed that she hadn't stuck to every one of her criteria, she was as thrilled to be at the new building as everyone else. It was a smoother relocation than anyone could have hoped for.

Then three months later, there was a tragedy in Gail's community: An entire office building quickly went up in flames, putting four substantial employers out of business. Guess which building it was? You got it — the one Gail thought was the perfect property.

Lesson learned. A business saved.

Intuition in All Realms

The Unexpected Decision

By all accounts, Garrett was a practical guy, never doing anything that anyone else would consider shocking or unexpected. Some called him dull, but he thought of himself as practical. And he didn't mind his life. It resonated well with him. He went to college in the town he grew up in, now worked in that same town, and even lived in the same house he grew up in.

Despite his seemingly lackluster life, Garrett was a really interesting guy to talk to when you got to know him, and he was also a stellar artist. And he had a great sense of humor. He was a bit shy, but in a way that actually made him quite fascinating. So when his small circle of friends found out what he'd done, they were completely shocked.

Garrett had taken a job in a different city, which was ten hours away. He would be selling the home he grew up in and moving. "A 45-year-old guy just doesn't do that." People wrote it off as a midlife crisis, and expected him to change his mind. He didn't.

But what really shocked people from his hometown was learning that Garrett was going to be on the cover of a magazine for local artists. He'd gotten a job designing some pieces for a steampunk movie.

When his friends asked him how this opportunity had come about, he smiled sheepishly and said, "I just kept having the feeling that I was meant to do it. I didn't want to tell anyone, because you'd have thought I was crazy."

They laughed. Rest assured, his friends grew envious of his ability to follow his gut instinct, and not make excuses to hold himself back. It led to some exciting inspiration in others, too!

Too Shy to Try

Being shy is never easy for anyone, but for Sandy, it was really painful at times. When she was at work, she would keep to herself, feeling envious of the camaraderie that her coworkers had with each other. When she was out at busy stores, Sandy was the one who would let everyone butt in front of her without even saying "excuse me." At her apartment building, she just walked in the front door, got her mail, and went up to her apartment.

Every night, she'd think: *I have got to make a point to try more tomorrow.*

Every tomorrow, she'd put it off for another day.

At her workplace, there was an attractive guy who would always say "hi" to her. She'd freak out every time, because she didn't even know what "boring old her" would say to him. Everyone liked him. Yet she always passed on actually talking to him.

Early one morning, Sandy was in the breakroom making coffee and thinking: *Today's the day.* She breathed in and smiled, having a temporary burst of courage, which was easy to do when no one else was around.

"Good morning, Sandy," someone said.

She knew the voice. She'd heard it often enough. It was his voice. She said, "Hi." Of course, she'd always gotten a "Hi" out before, but this one was considerably louder.

Then she stopped thinking about everything so intensely, and she took action. She turned around and smiled.

"How are you today?" he asked.

I can do this, she thought. "Good, and you?"

"Great," he said.

She smiled, grabbed her coffee, and walked away. But she'd done it. It was simple, and it hadn't killed her!

Sandy's desire to break the bad habit had finally been boosted by an intuitive act.

And this small step created a snowball effect. A few small words led to more words, actual conversations with other employees, and eventually moving into a management role. As for the guy, he moved to a different company, which was great, because it cleared the way for him to date her.

One small act of intuitive courage can lead to more amazing things than anyone can predict!

Activating Your Full-Circle Intuition

Now that we're full-circle, this last exercise is going to be full, all-out fun. It's going to be simple: You're going to build your ideal intuition-based scenario, which will help you in every area of your life — small and large. This scenario may not be the way it actually all goes down for you, but it's guaranteed to generate some excitement about what could potentially take place.

Here's why it will be so exciting:

- ✓ You thought of it.
- ✓ You created it.
- ✓ You fulfilled it.
- ✓ It is actually you!

What's one thing that you've dreamt of doing in your life? What would you really love to do? Get as far out of your comfort zone as necessary, but keep in mind that it needs to be something that's doable, even if you're not quite ready to do it yet!

_____

_____

_____

What's the very first step you must take to accomplish this goal?

_____

_____

_____

Do you already have any intuition in play to take this step? If yes, what is it? If no, what do you need to focus on? (HINT: The answer will be the same for both questions.)

_____

_____

_____

List a series of seven steps or strategies that you must take to begin making this goal happen:

1. _____

2. _____

3. _____

4. _____

5. _____

6. _____

7. _____

What does your intuition tell you about ways to accomplish this goal?

_____

_____

_____

Write down a visualization for making this goal happen. Remember to utilize the steps and reminders from all the chapters, and use as much detail as possible. You'll probably need another piece of paper, because there isn't enough space here!

_____
_____
_____

What will happen after you fulfill this goal?

_____
_____
_____

What's your reward?

_____
_____

How does this reward help you view the future more optimistically?

_____
_____

What skills have you gained that make your success goggles feel a bit wiser?

_____
_____

What lessons have you learned that help your intuition work more favorably for you?

_____
_____

Realizing that you've got this, describe how you're feeling at this moment:

_____

_____

What strengths will help you live a 3 Second Rule way of life?

_____

_____

You've taken amazing steps, but you're not flying solo yet. I'm here for you, and I've shared the ideas that I've used to apply these teachings to my own life. If you follow the steps in the next chapter, you'll improve even further, and intuition will begin to show in your life in incredible ways. Are you willing to do the work that will make it happen?

CHAPTER ELEVEN

3-Month Commitment

If you really commit to changing the level of intuition you operate on, you'll experience changes. The 3-month plan below is designed to walk you through the process of building your bridge to intuition and creating authentic, sustainable changes. These changes will elevate you to a new, more desirable way of living.

After the construction is complete, you'll be one of the success stories from the Full-Circle Intuition chapter. It's not always the noticeably big accomplishments (such as starting a Fortune 500 company) that have the biggest impact. It can also be the small things, such as creating a better culture for your family. If you're in touch with your intuition, the people around you will start getting in touch with theirs. It's absolutely contagious!

How to use this evaluation guide:

Your monthly evaluation process shouldn't be intensively long. But it should ensure that you keep working on building that bridge, and working toward a life that has all the benefits of intuition and the 3 Second Rule.

Here's what you want to commit to doing:

1. At the beginning of each month, allot one hour to working on your evaluation for that month.
2. Get out your calendar, and mark the hour you're going to allot.
3. Make sure that you create this plan while you're alone and uninterrupted.
4. Consider getting input from those closest to you. Ask them if they've seen any adjustments in what you've been doing, or the results you've delivered. While the opinions of others should never trump your own, other people are wonderful ways to gauge how much your internal changes are manifesting in an external way.

Month 1: Acknowledgment, Action, Self-Awareness

Acknowledgment

What have you learned about yourself this month that surprises you the most?

_____

_____

Have you recognized or pinpointed any undesirable habits and tendencies that you're focused on changing? If yes, what are they? If no, do you believe you've been fair about your self-evaluation?

_____

_____

What struggles are you having about honestly acknowledging and assessing the person you are?

_____

_____

What solutions could help you get through those struggles? Are the solutions good for your long-term growth strategies?

_____

_____

What part of acknowledging who you are has been the most exciting for you? Why?

_____

_____

Action

You are taking action — whether or not you're choosing to aggressively go out and do something, or to sit back and let everyone else reveal the path. Are you utilizing active, passive, or fear-based actions? Keeping those in mind, how would you describe your efforts this past month?

_____

_____

Have you improved, gotten worse, or stayed the same since you began implementing the 3 Second Rule in your life?

_____

_____

What type of person-of-action have you committed to becoming?

_____

_____

Thus far, what have you done that proves that you're really working toward this type of action in your life?

_____

_____

Self-Awareness

When we're self-aware, we're able to catch ourselves in the moment, and better understand why we're acting in a certain manner. With that understanding, what has caught you most off-guard in the past month?

_____

_____

In regard to your responses to situations, do you feel you've learned, grown, or changed? How?

_____

_____

Do you like what you're learning about yourself in this transition? Why or why not?

_____

_____

In the future, will you get better at becoming more self-aware?

1. Yes
2. No

Month 2: Desires, Drive, and Discipline

It's the end of Month 2. You must be feeling excited about the progress you've made. Even if you've only made a small amount of progress toward a successful transition into the 3 Second Rule, you've come a long way. How do I know? Because a little intuition goes a long way, and so does knowing yourself better!

Desires

What surprises you the most about everything you've learned about your pattern of desires in the past?

_____

_____

How have your desires begun to shift?

_____

_____

After the second month of implementing the 3 Second Rule, what is your greatest desire?

_____

_____

What are you doing to achieve it?

_____

_____

Drive

There are always going to be some things that we're more eager to do than others. Regarding this process (such as learning to implement the 3 Second Rule in your life), what do you think of the drive you've demonstrated?

_____

_____

Could you make improvements? How?

_____

_____

At this point, do you believe that the 3 Second Rule is able to work for you? Why?

_____

_____

What plans do you have in place to keep your "drive alive"?

_____

_____

What are the three most exciting benefits of experiencing the drive to succeed, especially when success means recognizing the value of intuition?

1. _____

2. _____

3. _____

Discipline

You've been trying to think of discipline as an exciting tool to help you achieve the reward of intuition. Thus far, how would you describe your journey toward this goal?

_____

_____

What do you love most about having discipline? How does this benefit make you feel?

_____

_____

What are your greatest struggles with discipline?

_____

_____

How have you taken action to resolve those struggles?

_____

_____

On a scale of 1 to 10 (10 being the most disciplined), how would you rate your discipline?

_____

_____

Month 3: Evaluation, Fulfillment, and Full-Circle Intuition

Right now, you may have already crossed that bridge, or perhaps you're on the cusp of it. But it's been such a great journey!

Evaluation

What do you know now, that you didn't know when you began the process of building your bridge to intuition?

_____

_____

What's been your greatest high?

_____

_____

What's been your toughest low?

_____

_____

What do you think are your three strongest evaluation skills?

1. _____
2. _____
3. _____

How has acknowledging and using these skills changed your life for the better?

_____
_____

Fulfillment

When we feel fulfilled, we cannot help but recognize our blessings more easily, so we manage our conflicts with a steadier hand. Remember, every challenge does not create a doomsday. What has your response been to the wonderful things in your life?

_____
_____

Now you've experienced fulfillment, and you have an intuition-based point of view. At this point, what have you learned about how you respond to challenging situations?

_____
_____

What ideas do you have about halting anything that's distracting you from using your intuition to continue living a fulfilled life?

_____
_____

Describe what fulfillment feels like to you:

_____

_____

Full-Circle Intuition

When you really experience an "aha moment", say to
yourself, "Oh, that's what it's like." After you do, you'll
reach full-circle intuition. What's been the most exciting
part of this journey for you?

_____

_____

Have others commented on something different about
you — even if they can't quite pinpoint what it is? What
did they say?

_____

_____

What are the most exciting differences you've noticed in
the daily grind of your life? And what are your responses
to it?

_____

_____

How do you see your future playing out differently, now
that you're living in or nearing full-circle intuition?

_____

_____

Compare the Quizzes

You took this quiz at the beginning of this book. Now
it's time to take it again, and see how different your

responses are today. If you think you aren't quite ready, wait another month to take it. To check yourself, you might even take this quiz once a year. Remember how important self-evaluation is to personal growth!

1. Do you believe that your life can be easy, and you can still do everything you want?
   a. Yes
   b. No

2. How aware are you of what you're genuinely feeling at any moment?
   a. I know, but if I don't want to deal with it, I avoid it.
   b. I just go with the flow, and don't really pay attention other than that.
   c. I am the most confused person I know.
   d. Honestly, I have no idea. I don't really focus on that type of thing very often.

3. When you think about the current level of trust you have in your decision-making abilities, which of these choices seems most accurate?
   a. I always run into trouble by making the wrong choice.
   b. My ability to make a sound choice is pretty decent.
   c. More often than not, I talk myself into trusting the choices I make.

d. I just do what I want, and don't put much thought into it.

How do you feel about your answer? Do you like or dislike it? Why?

_____

_____

4. Something <u>urgent</u> needs to be done. What are you most likely to do?
   a. Take care of it immediately. After all, it needs your attention.
   b. Put it on your priority list in the proper place, according to the order in which you want to deal with it.
   c. Procrastinate, for whatever reason.
   d. Dwell and contemplate, but don't act for a long time. If it's urgent, you want to take your time.

5. Something that's <u>not urgent</u> needs to be done. What are you most likely to do?
   a. Put it off as long as you can.
   b. Do it right away, because it's not challenging.
   c. Keep forgetting about it. There are too many other fires to put out.
   d. Put it in the proper spot on your priority list.

How do you feel about the differences between urgent action and non-urgent action?

_____

_____

6. You're faced with a task, and there are two ways to accomplish it. Choice One is the easy way: You're cutting a few corners, but saving a ton of time. Choice Two is doing it the right way, so you don't ever have to go back and redo it?

    a. Choice One: Get it done. And if it comes back to bite you, you'll deal with it at that time.

    b. Choice Two: Do it right the first time, and move on to the next thing.

    If you selected Choice One, what outcome usually happens? And how do you feel about it?

    _____

    _____

7. Something new comes up in your life, and you have to decide if you're going to pursue it or take a pass. How do you feel about your ability to evaluate your decision-making process?

    a. Pretty great. I analyze, do research, sleep on it, and do a second run-through. Then I'm ready for action.

    b. If I have any hesitation, it's an automatic no.

    c. If it sounds interesting, I'm all in.

    d. I say yes right away, then dive into the details later, especially if it involves a financial gain of some sort.

8. What do you do when you want something really badly, and can't stop thinking about it?

    a. Create a plan to obtain it, then obtain it.

b. Create a plan to obtain it, but usually lose interest along the way.

c. Dwell on it and daydream about it, but don't ever really "go for it."

d. Think it's such a long shot that it's not worth my time. Case closed.

When was the last time you got something that you really desired, either big or small? How did that feel for you?

_____

_____

9. How far are you willing to go in life to get what you want?

a. The distance.

b. Not too far.

c. Far enough to see if it's worth it.

d. I'm too busy to even consider pursuing most things.

10. Having discipline is something that's not easy at times, so it can present a challenge, even to the most successful individual. What about you? What do you do?

a. Feel that it's okay to take some time off and recharge.

b. Make sure I work toward what I want every day, regardless.

c. Find it easy to be disciplined when I'm busy, but not as easy when I don't have a full schedule.

Evaluate your disciplinary behaviors. Regarding discipline, what are your strengths, and where could you use some improvement?

_____

_____

11. When you think about yourself, what do you do?
    a. Focus on failures first, then successes.
    b. Focus on successes, then the lessons learned from failures.
    c. Only think about the failures.
    d. Only think about the successes.

12. If you were giving advice to a friend who had identical mannerisms to you, what would you do?
    a. Be very kind to them, even if it wasn't the best advice.
    b. Be direct and gentle, and really try to be helpful, even if it's tough.
    c. Just listen, and let them talk it out themselves.
    d. Directly tell them what you think they should do, without exception.

In your own experience, how do you feel about offering advice? And how about receiving it (both solicited and unsolicited)?

_____

_____

13. Regardless of how busy you are, do you feel that your actions add up to a more fulfilling life?

    a. All the time. I love the life I've chosen, bumps and joys alike.

    b. Most of the time. But there are times when I've got to wonder: *What was I thinking?*

    c. Never. I've gotten it wrong so many times that I'm not even sure what being right feels like anymore.

    d. Thinking about it is too irritating, so I choose not to.

14. What would you do if everything started going your way — to the point where you couldn't ignore that things were "clicking?"

    a. Wonder when it is going to end.

    b. Seize the day.

    c. Hide out because you fear the sky is falling.

    d. Think it's a cruel joke.

That wasn't so bad, was it? Now it's time to find out *exactly* where you are at this moment in time. Keep in mind that the smallest strides toward building the bridge to your intuition can significantly change your life. Just as the ripples from tossing a pebble into the water grow bigger, so does the smallest change that takes you one step closer to your intuition.

Now add up your scores again:

1. a-2; b-1
2. a-4; b-3; c-2; d-1
3. a-1; b-3; c-2; d-4
4. a-3; b-4; c-2; d-1
5. a-1; b-4; c-2; d-3
6. a-2; b-1
7. a-3; b-4; c-1; d-2
8. a-4; b-1; c-3; d-2
9. a-3; b-2; c-4; d-1
10. a-1; b-3; c-2
11. a-3; b-4; c-2; d-1
12. a-1; b-4; c-3; d-2
13. a-3; b-4; c-1; d-2
14. a-3; b-4; c-1; d-2

Add up your score, and take note of it. Remember, 51 is the maximum score you can get.

48 and Above: My Bridge is Half-Built

Congratulations, not bad! You have some sound, intuitive building blocks in place. If you get tripped up, it most likely comes from a lack of confidence and a sense of perfectionism.

40 through 47: Riding the Fence

You're onto something, but not quite there. You run about 50/50, in terms of allowing your instincts to work for you. The largest challenge you may face is having a strong self-will, as well as a splash of too much ego.

30 through 39: Belly Flop

You try to get ahead. But more often than not, you accidentally topple over, and fall flat on your face. But to your credit, you get back up again, and maintain hope. You just have to focus on learning from your mistakes and creating an evaluation process.

29 and Below: Build the Ladder Before the Bridge

First, breathe deeply, and acknowledge that you have amazing potential for gaining the right instincts. What's lacking is an acceptance of that part of you underneath the surface. It's there. It truly is! Revisit the chapters, and take some more time to soak in the book's meaning. It's not about rushing to intuition. Instead, think of it as a meaningful journey that starts the process to bridge the gap and jump-start your life. Exciting stuff!

Now ask yourself...

- ✓ Am I better now than I was when I first took this quiz?
- ✓ If I didn't improve, why?
- ✓ Is this the highest score I'm likely to have?
- ✓ What am I willing to do to increase my score?

Make a plan to take action, then repeat the quiz in six months.

Conclusion

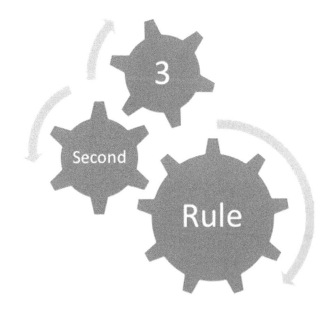

Can you believe how much you've learned from this book? I certainly hope it's had a life-changing impact on you. The intention behind all this wisdom is good, and I'm truly sincere about you having the potential to apply these steps to your life, create a bridge that links you to intuition, and actualize the 3 Second Rule way of living.

I learned all that I've shared with you through a combination of personal experience, inspiration, and (most importantly) action. I have no special formula here, and I didn't start out with an edge. It all began quite deliberately. Today, I'm working in a field that I love. I'm more fully able to tap into my own creativity, and I bring people inventions and books that are designed to inspire, innovate, and motivate. It doesn't get any better than that!

Let's recap what you've learned. If you ever need a quick refresher, just refer back to this conclusion. Sometimes, you need a little reminder about what the good fight really is: It's the fight for embracing your intuition, which is the protector of your behavior. Intuition is a guiding force for good in you, and by extension, a force for good in the people you love and the world around you. Who could argue with that?

Step 1 | The Starting Point
This step is the first building block in your bridge to intuition. It gives you an intuitive starting point.

Step 2 | Acknowledgment
This step helps you tap into the answers to these three important questions:

- ✓ What do I say?
- ✓ What do I do?
- ✓ How do I feel?

By focusing on these three questions, you gain a stronger perspective about where you are in life, and the doorway to your full potential has opened up. Maybe it reveals a long journey, or maybe you find out you're already halfway down the road to intuition. Either way, you discover your ability to acknowledge your current place. The best part? You reveal where you have the potential to go.

Step 3 | Action

The fundamental message of this step is understanding the importance of action in everything we do. Action involves understanding our responses to life, which is why we tapped into the following three building blocks:

- ✓ Active response
- ✓ Passive behavior
- ✓ Fear-driven digression

Knowing how we respond to life's events is important, regardless of how big they seem. Our actions determine our outcomes. Likewise, our actions can either create opportunities, or leave the call to opportunity unanswered.

Step 4 | Self-Awareness

The person we are isn't always the person we're capable of becoming. You can either create the best version of yourself, or settle for something less. The choice is yours. That's how the building blocks show how self-aware you are:

- ✓ Confidence
- ✓ Understanding
- ✓ Defined, relatable goals

For the most part, we're passionate and emotional beings — even the "driest" of us. It's fundamentally important that we understand where our emotions come from, since this understanding develops the 3 Second Rule way of living. Then we'll discover the ways they contribute to our results.

Step 5 | Desires

The heart wants what it wants. Learning why we desire is important, but it's even more important to harness the energy that desire brings us. This energy keeps the drive to intuition moving forward. The building blocks of this chapter include:

- ✓ Excitement
- ✓ Energy
- ✓ Ambitions

We can feel alive, accepted, and accomplished (according to our own definition of these words) by learning where we stand in relation to these building blocks, and combining this information with our truest desires.

Step 6 | Drive

Our minds are the engines that drive our entire bodies, both physically and metaphysically. Therefore, we need to know how to maintain this important engine. As we pursue a higher level of intuition, the building blocks in this chapter give us insight into the power of our minds. We must factor in the following:

- ✓ Resilience levels
- ✓ Alertness
- ✓ Motivating factors for your life

When you have drive, you learn what you need to do, and obtain the discipline you need to do it. Then your instincts kick in, and help you take the most effective, beneficial steps. And the journey doesn't have to tire you out, either. Instead, you can feel invigorated!

Step 7 | Discipline

Every day, you make decisions. Yes, you have things that must get done. However, there is still plenty of time left over to do what you want. In this case, you want to develop a higher level of intuition.

The three building blocks to be aware of include:

- ✓ Understanding your values.
- ✓ Being a person of principle.
- ✓ Gaining the ability to focus on what you want to do.

By being the most active, engaged participant in your life that you possibly can, there are no limits to what you can do. Knowing yourself is inspiring and effective, and it allows you to demonstrate how effective discipline can be.

Step 8 | Evaluation

As your instincts develop, you start taking actions that will revolutionize your thought processes and outcomes. But you can't just start "winging it" again. Rather, you need to evaluate. Evaluation is the only way to gauge what has been working, what hasn't been working, and why.

To accomplish these goals, you need to focus on three things:

- ✓ Practicality
- ✓ Applicability
- ✓ Do-ability

No one is tougher on you than you are. That's why engaging in evaluation is important. It helps you experience successful outcomes. Here's what I love best about evaluation: It allows you to find out whether your ego is still running your mind, and if you've truly invited your natural intuition back into your life.

Step 9 | Fulfillment

This last building block completes your bridge, and it is every bit the cherry on the sundae. In fact, it is the exclamation point when you shout, "YES!" The toughest challenges and journeys are often the most rewarding. And if you didn't feel fulfillment from them, you would be doing yourself a great disservice.

Fulfillment stems from these three building blocks:

- ✓ Knowing the reward
- ✓ Completing the vision
- ✓ Gaining peace from success

Step 10 | Fulfillment

Intuition makes every area of your life better, because it's always working for you, even when you aren't paying attention. If you don't fight it, intuition gives you the strength and knowledge to move mountains, and guides you down the path to success. Then you win in your personal life and your professional life. And most importantly, you feel like a better, more fulfilled person.

After you go through the work to gain intuitive skills (which are intensive for some, but only challenging for others), you need to really begin living by the 3 Second Rule. Then you're going to realize a few things:

1. *You've done it!* You have an elite mindset, and you can actually trust your intuition. You understand who you are, and why you're that person. And you know that there are sources of insight, which are greater than your conscious mind.

2. *You've experienced it!* When all these ideas, strategies, and commitments pay off, you'll have one of the sweetest tastes of success that you could ever imagine. In fact, you'll become possessive about it. Then you'll naturally take steps to protect your intuition, and make sure that you never abandon it again.

3. *You'll live in full-circle intuition!* Through effortless trust in your intuition, you'll learn to accept your decisions with fewer regrets and

higher levels of confidence. Do these decisions always make sense in your conscious mind? Maybe not, but you won't lie awake at night, wondering if you made the right decision. You'll just *know* that you made the right choice! Sleep gives you energy, which increases your quality of life, and drives you to give all areas of your life your best. And here's the secret: You'll automatically start experiencing better things, too!

Are you ready to start a discussion in your mind?

Has the time come to reconnect with your intuition? If it has, then you can give yourself a break. I believe it has, and there is evidence throughout this vast world that people are all seeking something to help them reach the ultimate level of fulfillment and accomplishment in their lives. Intuition can take you there. It's no coincidence that intuition is free, and available to everyone from all walks of life. And it will work favorably for you and will never harm anyone else.

It's time to get started. The countdown is on. The 3 Second Rule way of life has now officially been activated in your life!

APPENDIX A

Affirmations

On the website yourdictionary.com, affirmations are defined as "the act of confirming something to be true, or a written or oral statement that confirms something is true." That definition holds such power! When you think about your life, determine the following: Do you lift yourself up through positive self-talk, or do you tend to distract or dissuade yourself from achieving what you don't understand?

Through the use of affirmations, you're given a tool that allows your subconscious mind to be fed positive thoughts that help transform your outcomes — from your deepest level outward. Experts believe that affirmations are intricate parts of every person's growth. They fuel your thoughts with positive, motivational ideas about what you can do, and squash everything you cannot do. Here's the reason why affirmations were listed in every section of this book: They will help you apply the 3 Second Rule to your own life. Intuition thrives off of positive affirmations, just as it starves due to negative affirmations. (Yes, negative affirmations do exist.)

If you're not familiar with affirmations and the ways to effectively use them, you'll soon begin to appreciate their power. You want to stop feeling disconnected from the results you receive, and you want to start feeling attuned to your outcomes. Affirmations are the perfect tools for helping with that transition.

Here are four things you should know about them:

- ✓ Affirmations help you conquer weaknesses or self-perceived inadequacies. You'll grow stronger, smarter, and closer to an intuitive way of living.
- ✓ All people need affirmations in their lives. They're fuel for the mind, and they help you accomplish the things that will really make a positive impact on you.
- ✓ Every person has the ability to effectively use affirmations if they choose to. No exceptions!
- ✓ Through the use of affirmations, you're strengthening your bridge to a 3 Second Rule way of life.

There's one basic rule that will help you understand how affirmations work: Accept that your thoughts are energy. Do you want them to be the fatty feast that leaves you feeling lazy and lethargic? Or do you want them to be the healthy banquet that gives you an abundance of energy, so you can enjoy your life more fully? Go for the healthy buffet, of course!

If you do, here's what you have to gain:

✓ *Better tools to sort and process life's challenges.* Affirmations don't alleviate tough situations, but they can help equip you with ways to handle them more proficiently — and with fewer cripplingly negative emotions.

✓ *Reminders that inspire you to take action and achieve what you desire.* Affirmations don't make great things happen. But they do prepare your mind to accept that they will — and to seek out the opportunities to make them happen.

✓ *A system for reminding yourself that good intentions lead to good results.* You're going to feel a natural sense of optimism that inspires action. In turn, this optimism will create greater happiness, better results, closer relationships, and greater service to others and your community.

Learning to use affirmations is key, whether you're creating them for small changes or large, substantial ones. And it's simple: It all goes back to the earlier insight about creating habits. If you commit to it, it'll happen, and it'll become second nature.

Follow these tips:

- ✓ *Claim it.* Speak and think your affirmations, as if they've already happened.
- ✓ *Focus on you.* You cannot affirm others into positive thinking. You can only lead by example.
- ✓ *Use detailed visualizations.* There's nothing more powerful than seeing yourself in the moment, even if you haven't lived it yet. For example, envision yourself recognizing a bad investment opportunity after one comes your way. You know that you can pass on it, and that things will be okay. If you miss out on something great, that's okay, too. Your intuition serves your best interests far more than they'll ever work against you. In other words, your intuition is innately good, and it guides you to good things.
- ✓ *Take action.* Nice thoughts are only effective if they're followed by good, sound actions that bring them to fruition. Remember, thinking without acting is just hoping.
- ✓ *Be careful not to allow any negative or limiting words and thoughts into your mind.* They have no place in an affirmation. Here are the banned phrases:
  - Am not.
  - Can't (or cannot).
  - Don't (or do not).
  - Won't (or will not).

Instead, use phrases that are based on achieving with confidence:

- I am.
- I will.
- This is.
- I can.

✓ *Allow repetition to be your friend.* Many people think the same old thoughts over and over again. If you're a repetitive thinker, make sure you're repeating positive thoughts. No past baggage, no regrets, no resentments. You can either say your affirmations once a day or several times a day. You can say your affirmations first thing in the morning, throughout the day, before you go to sleep, or whenever you recognize you're slipping away from positivity.

✓ *When you're in motion, try contemplating and stating your affirmations.* This method helps you ingrain the message. For example, many people try this method when they're exercising or driving.

✓ *Keep affirming until it comes true.* Some people call this method "Fake It Till You Make It." And that's okay to do when you're trying to achieve something good!

Over the years, I've used affirmations for many things, with great results. Stressful times are now less stressful, because I'm more rooted in the belief that everything will work out. Challenges become opportunities to learn. And the smallest joys in life — as well as the large, wonderful surprises — are more easily recognized, which is good. And I want you to benefit from affirmations, too!

About Douglas Shawn Blakeny II

Douglas Shawn Blakeny II (known as Shawn to friends) has lived an inspired life, rising from the depths of Youngtown, Ohio and tapping into the entrepreneur in him early on, with the support of a mother and father who reminded him and his sisters that they should always reach for their best potential. He has always taken his parents' lesson to heart.

Growing up, Shawn recognized that he had an affinity for coming up with ideas and concepts that he thought could add value to others' lives in some way, whether it be helping them learn something beneficial, putting a smile on their faces, or inspiring them to achieve their own greatness. The result has been a career that has sparked his greatest passions: Inventing and being an author. According to Shawn, "I'm always thinking of something new, and trying to find ways to bring it to market."

When it comes to his written works, there's a constant desire to get all the ideas out that are in his head and put them onto paper, so they can be published. It's not about saying you have a book on Amazon or at Barnes & Noble; it's about helping better other people's lives in some way. This concept holds true for both his works of fiction and nonfiction.

Shawn is also a highly active guy, particularly enjoying the Cavs and Indians, and watching other sports on TV.

He's recently started golfing, quickly realizing that there's a good reason that golf instructors exist! He also enjoys spending time at the shooting range and traveling. And he benefits from a regular workout routine, which is a great way to keep his ideas flowing and maintain high-paced energy for his on-the-go lifestyle.

The people in Shawn's life have had a great impact on deciding which charities and causes he likes to support. In 2010, his mother most unexpectedly passed away from a brain aneurysm. So he now supports the Brain Aneurysm Foundation, in order to help raise awareness about symptoms and potentially proactive solutions. And having helped people with autism transition into adulthood, Shawn is also a strong advocate for Autism Awareness.

Many people have been influential in Shawn's life, especially his mother. While she is no longer living, her hopes and dreams for Shawn's contributions continue to inspire him.

His father has also been a wonderful inspiration for Shawn, as he's helped guide Shawn to make better choices and avoid the same mistakes that he made in his youth. His father's continued emphasis on being the best he could be — academically, athletically, and as a man — have helped Shawn develop the foundation for his work ethic, discipline, and greatest joys.

Shawn's supporting cast includes his sisters and stepmother. In a world where many people come and go, he's always found a way to grow and be inspired by the friends and family he has around him. And he is grateful for their continued support and belief in him.